MW01028379

The Shaking of Adventism

GEOFFREY J. PAXTON

BAKER BOOK HOUSE
Grand Rapids, Michigan

Reprinted 1978 by Baker Book House
with permission of copyright owner

ISBN: 0-8010-7034-1

First printing, February 1978
Second printing, April 1978

PHOTOLITHOPRINTED BY CUSHING - MALLOY, INC.
ANN ARBOR, MICHIGAN, UNITED STATES OF AMERICA
1978

This book is dedicated to
Helen, Nigel, and Simon.

Preface

This book approaches Adventism from a perspective which has not been adopted before. In this respect it may modestly claim the appellation, "original." The book seeks to "get inside the skin" of the Adventist and look at his movement from that vantage point.

This book had its first form in a thesis presented to the Department of Studies in Religion within the University of Queensland, Australia. It is only fitting, then, that I should thank my supervisor, Rev. Dr. Ian Gillman, Th.D., who never said he was too busy and indulged me at times when I knew it was difficult for him to do so. Also, I should thank Miss Denise F. Scott, L.Th., B.D., for her tireless effort in typing and retyping the manuscript.

The book is sent out in the hope that it will be a contribution to Seventh-day Adventists from a sympathetic critic and will lead to better understanding among Christian people.

Geoffrey J. Paxton

Contents

Introduction 11

Part I: Adventism and the Reformation
1. Adventists: Heirs of the Reformation 17
2. The Heart of the Reformation 35

Part II: Adventism before 1950
3. Off to an Inauspicious Start: 1844-1888 53
4. Attempted Breakthrough: 1888-1950 63

Part III: Adventism after 1950
5. Off to an Auspicious Start: The 1950's 85
6. Pain and Progress: The 1960's 105
7. Advance and Retreat: The 1970's 121

Conclusion: The Shaking of Adventism 147
Bibliography 159
Index of Seventh-day Adventist Persons 171

Introduction

This is not a general book about Seventh-day Adventism. Rather, it is an examination of the real heart of the movement — namely, its conviction that *those within it constitute God's special last-day propagators of the gospel in such a way as to make them the only true heirs of the Reformers*.

From this perspective, the first section opens with an analysis of Seventh-day Adventists and their claim to be the special heirs of the Reformation. Then the heart of the Reformation itself is elucidated with the purpose of establishing the norm that will be used to judge the Adventist claim.

The second section looks at the way the gospel was handled by Adventism prior to 1950. However, since the main focus of the book is on the modern period, the 1844-1950 era is not dealt with exhaustively. Instead, the major trends and developments are presented as concisely as is consistent with accuracy.

The third section, covering the years from 1950 to the present, is the main part of the book. The three decades included in this period furnish the reader with helpful divisions, since they conveniently coincide with the actual stages of development in Adventism. A primary object of this section is to let the historical facts speak for themselves. I have resisted a personal evaluation until the conclusion.

The title, *The Shaking of Adventism*, will be highly significant to Seventh-day Adventists. They will think of the eschatological "shaking" through which they understand the church must pass before she finally accomplishes her mission. As the editors of the general church paper, the *Review and Herald*, have recently pointed out,[1] this concept and expectation of shaking is deeply rooted in the Adventist consciousness. Further, it is also believed that the shaking will take place over the concept of righteousness by faith.

The reader may wonder why I have not appraised the work of Ellen G. White on this subject.[2] I have thought it best to confine myself to the way the general body of the movement in North America and Australia has handled the gospel of the Reformation. Besides that, it has become clear to me that Adventists are divided on how they ought to read Mrs. White on this topic. Why should I attempt to explain such a controverted area when they are not agreed on it themselves? For a non-Adventist Protestant, the facts concerning the way Adventists treat the gospel *today* must speak for themselves. It is up to Adventists to decide whether the way they have spoken of the gospel is true to Mrs. White or not.

Frequent footnotes have been included to enable the reader to check the foundations for the things I say. This book is a serious attempt to evaluate the heart of the movement rather than to deal with side issues, irrespective of how important they might be in a more general treatment.

---

1. See *Review and Herald*, 16 June 1977, p. 11; 30 June 1977, p. 2; 7 July 1977, p. 2.

2. Mrs. Ellen G. White (1827-1915) helped found the Seventh-day Adventist Church in the middle of the last century. As a charismatic leader, she is recognized by Seventh-day Adventists as "the Lord's messenger" who gave the Lord's counsel and guidance to the fledgling church.

Part I

Adventism and the Reformation

1

Adventists:
Heirs of the Reformation

Seventh-day Adventists have been very misunderstood. The reasons for this are no doubt complex. But whatever the reasons, the fact remains that most critiques of Adventism have failed to reach the heart of the matter. Adventists have often had trouble recognizing themselves in such analyses.

The impression that Seventh-day Adventism is little better than a non-Christian sect will not stand close examination. Adventists believe in the Holy Trinity, the deity of Christ, the virgin birth, the sinless life and atoning sacrifice of Christ on the cross, and His bodily resurrection and ascension to the right hand of the Father. This is not the creed of a non-Christian sect. Furthermore, Seventh-day Adventists believe in salvation by grace through faith alone as fervently as do most evangelicals. They believe in sanctification by the indwelling Holy Spirit and in the soon return of Jesus Christ in great power and glory. No, whatever we think of this or that Adventist "distinctive," we have to recognize the movement as being *Christian*.

It is sometimes said that Seventh-day Adventists claim salvation by Sabbath-keeping. But in my contact with them, I have never once heard this. Adventists do not believe they are accepted by God because they keep the Sabbath any more than they believe they are accepted by God because they practice monogamy!

If Adventists are regarded as Christian, they are often thought of as those who "major on minors." But those Adventists who have given support to this accusation can hardly be seen as faithful to the heartthrob of the Adventist mission. In fact, when viewed in the light of the real Adventist claim, this accusation will be seen as wide of the mark.

The Adventist Claim

What, then, is the *real* Adventist claim? How does he see his mission here on earth? What does he see as his reason for existence?

The Adventist views himself as standing in the line of the Protestant Reformation. He regards himself as *Protestant* in the truest sense of the word. Where other Christians would not claim to stand in the line of the sixteenth-century Reformers, the Adventist is in no doubt about it. He is a son of Luther and Calvin.

That, however, is not all. In fact, it is hardly the beginning. At this point some of us evangelical-Reformed Christians might be in for a shock. Yet the fact is that the Seventh-day Adventist sees himself as standing in a unique relation to the Reformation. He believes that God has called him to carry forward the message of the Reformation *in such a way as no other Christian or Christian body is able to do*. In his opinion the Seventh-day Adventist is God's *special* heir of the Reformers. *Only* through the Adventist Church can the work of the Reformation be carried to its God-designed end.

Obviously, the existence of such a stupendous claim will require verification. As far as Adventists are concerned, we could hardly commence with a more prestigious testimony than that of Mrs. Ellen G. White. Mrs. White saw the Adventist movement as standing in the line of Luther and Calvin and, of course, Paul before them.

In her sizeable work, *The Great Controversy*, Mrs. White views the great battle between Christ and Satan as stretching from the antecedents of the Reformation (in such men as Huss and Wycliffe), through the Reformers themselves and their battle against Rome, to the Puritans and Wesley, and finally to the Seventh-day Adventist movement itself. Mrs. White writes:

Thus the Waldenses witnessed for God centuries before the birth of

Luther. Scattered over many lands, they planted the seeds of the Reformation that began in the time of Wycliffe, grew broad and deep in the days of Luther, and is to be carried forward to the close of time by those who also are willing to suffer all things for "the word of God, and for the testimony of Jesus Christ." Revelation 1:9.[1]

A frequent theme in Adventist writing and speaking is that of forwarding the Reformation. Mrs. White speaks of this as follows: "The Reformation did not, as many suppose, end with Luther. It is to be continued to the close of this world's history. Luther had a great work to do...."[2] Indeed, the Reformation did not end with Luther. It *will* end with the Adventist movement, however—at least as far as the Seventh-day Adventist is concerned. He believes that the challenge from God to be "willing to suffer all things for the word of God, and for the testimony of Jesus Christ" has come to his movement with unique force.

Mrs. White saw Luther as teaching the doctrine of justification by faith with brilliant clarity.[3] Luther was no inventor or innovator: "Christ was a protestant. ... Luther and his followers did not invent the reformed religion. They simply accepted it as presented by Christ and the apostles."[4] In such statements from Mrs. White it is clear that she saw neither herself nor Adventism in general as a "Johnny-come-lately" religious phenomenon. The movement was to receive and carry forward the torch of the everlasting gospel of the Reformation.

W. W. Prescott reinforces this perspective of Mrs. White. In the early years of this century Prescott edited an Adventist publication called *The Protestant Magazine*. It makes it clear that Adventists are the guardians of the Protestant heritage in a climate of modernism and spiritual declension. The magazine laments:

The departure of Protestantism from its original principles, and the acceptance of human philosophy in place of revealed truth, are giving to Romanism the opportunity to put forward with a greater show of plausibility the claim that the great Reformation was a

---

1. Ellen G. White, *The Great Controversy*, p. 78.
2. Ibid., p. 148.
3. Ibid., p. 253.
4. Ellen G. White, *Review and Herald*, 1 June 1886.

delusion and that the only stability of truth is found in the Roman communion.[5]

No apology is offered for the magazine's being a *Protestant* publication. Rather, it is said that the times demand such a magazine. The declaration made by the protesting princes at the Diet of Spires in 1529 is adopted as indicative of the magazine's stance.[6]

Carlyle B. Haynes published a work entitled *The Hour of God's Judgment* and included a chapter on "Completing the Unfinished Reformation."[7] Haynes carries on the line of reasoning which we found in Mrs. White. The great light of the gospel was given in the Reformation and handed down via the Puritans and Wesley to the little Adventist band in 1844.[8] The mission of the God-chosen torch bearers of 1844 is stated as follows:

> . . . in 1844, the time for the revelation of the fullness of gospel truth came. If the prophecy of Daniel eight be fulfilled, and assuredly it must be, then in 1844, we must confidently look for the beginning of a movement and a message which not only will complete an arrested Reformation, but also will disclose again to the knowledge of mankind all those truths which have been counterfeited during the centuries of the Middle Ages.
>
> To bear this message to the world, it was necessary that God institute another movement and raise up another people, separate from the established churches that had refused to walk in advancing light.[9]

Where has this Adventist conviction appeared in critiques of the movement? Has one really plumbed the depths of Adventism if this heart conviction has been bypassed?

---

5. *The Protestant Magazine* 1, no. 1 (2nd quarter, 1909): 1.

6. Ibid., pp. 32-6. The magazine carries an article entitled "The Rediscovery of a Vital Doctrine: Justification by Faith the Mainspring of the Great Reformation." In one place it says: "But this great doctrine of salvation proceeding from God and not from man, was not only the power of God to save Luther's soul; it became in a still greater degree the power of God to reform the Church, an effectual weapon wielded by the Apostles, —a weapon too long neglected, but taken at last, in all its primitive brightness, from the arsenal of the Omnipotent God. . . . It was in Rome that God gave him [Luther] this clear view of the fundamental doctrine of Christianity. . . . he brought away [from Rome] in his heart the salvation of the Church" (pp. 34, 36).

7. Carlyle B. Haynes, *The Hour of God's Judgment*, pp. 67-82.

8. See ibid., pp. 83-91. Here Haynes includes a chapter entitled "The Remnant Church and Its Message," which follows his chapter, "Completing the Unfinished Reformation."

9. Ibid., p. 78.

One of the most respected of Adventist scholars was LeRoy Edwin Froom, one-time Professor of Historical Theology at Andrews University, Berrien Springs, Michigan. He wrote some notable volumes which are respected not only in the Adventist movement, but outside the movement as well.[10] Froom smarted under the ignominy of his movement's being classified as a sect, and he labored to show its true catholicity. In the publication, *Our Firm Foundation*, he contributed a paper which was a digest of his much larger four-volume work, *Prophetic Faith of Our Fathers*. In this paper Dr. Froom sought to show that the Adventist prophetic interpretation is not an *innovation* but a *restoration* of the true historical position of the Reformers themselves. He writes as follows:

> In these latter days, as God's remnant workmen, we are called upon not only to reconstruct the Reformation edifice but to restore the early Church structure as well, and to bring everything into harmony with the divine Blueprint. We are even to restore original features omitted by the Reformers. And we are likewise to rebuild the parts distorted and rejected by the latter-day perverters of the Reformation positions. Not only are we confronted by this dual task, but we are commissioned to finish this uncompleted structure, carrying it through to consummation with the capstone of the present truth features of these latter days, thus bringing the full structure to completion.[11]

For Froom the bounden commission of the Advent movement is

> fundamentally a restoration, not the formation of a new structure. It is tied in inseparably with the efforts of all past builders of prophetic truth. ... we shall truly build again the foundations and superstructure of "many generations" into the stately edifice of truth originally designed by God. That is our bounden commission under the Advent movement.[12]

This stupendous consciousness of being special heirs of the historical Reformation position receives heightened expression when

---

10. *Prophetic Faith of Our Fathers*, *The Conditionalist Faith of Our Fathers*, *The Coming of the Comforter*, and *Movement of Destiny*.
11. LeRoy Edwin Froom, "The Advent Message Built upon the Foundations of Many Generations," in *Our Firm Foundation*, 2:81.
12. Ibid., p. 82.

Froom says: "... the floodlight of the world's pitiless scrutiny will soon be turned full upon us. ... More is demanded of us than our fathers and much more than our forefathers in generations past."[13] It is no coincidence that Froom concludes with words attributed to Martin Luther: "So, irrespective of others, here we stand, God helping us. We cannot do otherwise."[14]

More support for our thesis covering the fundamental conviction of Adventists would only prove tedious.[15] We will conclude this aspect of our examination with the words of Professor H. K. LaRondelle of Andrews University.[16] In his lectures on justification and sanctification in the fall of 1966, LaRondelle sums up the Adventist position as follows:

> Truly it can be said with LeRoy E. Froom, that the Advent movement after 1844 is the second great Reformation, continuing and completing the work of the first Reformation of the sixteenth century. The second Reformation, therefore, is not a revoking of the first Reformation, but on the contrary, its consummation, its recognition and perfection! If the first Reformation is the restoration of the Gospel with the saving doctrine of justification by faith alone, then the second Reformation is the restoration of the holy

---

13. Ibid., p. 83. One cannot fail to get the point when Froom says: "Herein lies our supreme opportunity of now stepping into our rightful place as the avowed restorers of the true Protestant positions of the founding fathers of all branches of Protestantism as it formerly obtained in all Protestant lands in both hemispheres. Instead of meekly accepting an unjust consignment to the ranks of modern heretics, as concerns our prophetic faith, we should humbly but effectively assert and establish, by sound reasoning and irrefutable evidence, our actual position as the champions and sustainers of the true, historical interpretations now regrettably abandoned by most of Protestantism's spiritual descendants. We should now rise to our full and allotted place as the revivers and continuers of the true Protestant interpretation of the Reformation. This is our rightful heritage. We are simply the last segment in God's sevenfold true church of the centuries. These former expositors of the true interpretations were of God's true church and were true expositors in their time. We are in the line of true succession" (pp. 99-100).

14. Ibid., p. 182.

15. E.g., "Is There a Relationship between Luther and Seventh-day Adventists," *The Ministry*, June 1955, pp. 39f. The article claims that both Lutheranism and Adventism are reform movements, both having been announced in Bible prophecy. Of Luther it says: "Justification by faith was to him the breath of life. It shaped his thinking." The article continues: "To Seventh-day Adventists this teaching of justification by faith is just as important."

16. Hans K. LaRondelle is Associate Professor of Systematic Theology at Andrews University. He studied for his doctorate under the famous Reformed theologian, G.C. Berkouwer, at the Free University of Amsterdam. LaRondelle received his doctorate for the dissertation, *Perfection and Perfectionism: A Dogmatic-Ethical Study of Biblical Perfection and Phenomenal Perfectionism*.

law of God in the doctrine of sanctification by faith and submission.[17]

Adventism and the Reformation Gospel

We have seen that the Seventh-day Adventist claims a unique relation to the Reformation. However, there is an important question to raise at this point: Exactly what is it that Adventists claim in the Reformation? Certainly they are not the only ones who give a positive appraisal of the Reformation or who claim the Reformers as their true parents.

Adventism has not adopted many aspects of the Reformation. Indeed, it would not wish to adopt many aspects. It has not adopted the Reformation mode of baptism, it has not adopted the Reformed form of church government, and it has not embraced the Lutheran view of the Supper. So again we ask, What is it to which Adventists lay claim in the Reformation?

We believe that the best way to answer this question is to ask and answer another question—a question of immense importance as far as the Seventh-day Adventist is concerned. It is a question which concerns the very heart of the movement. *What is it that Adventism believes it has to offer to the world? What is the contribution which, for one reason or another, it feels it is peculiarly equipped to make?* For the Adventist there can be but one answer: *the gospel!* Such an answer, of course, is deceptive in its simplicity. The answer may even be expressed in different ways. For example, it may be said that "righteousness by faith" is that which the Adventist has to offer to the world, or the "third angel's message."[18] But whatever terminology is used, the task which he believes he has received from God is to *continue* and to *consummate* the recovery of the

---

17. Hans K. LaRondelle, "Righteousness by Faith," p. 144.
18. The "third angel's message" is taken from the apocalyptic imagery of Rev. 14:9-12. Sometimes it is simply a "threefold message" (White, *Great Controversy*, p. 311). The first message is the everlasting gospel of the judgment of God (Rev. 14:6-7; idem, *Great Controversy*, pp. 453-54; idem, *Selected Messages*, 1:372). The second message announces the fall of Babylon (Rev. 14:8; idem, *Prophets and Kings*, pp. 677-78, 713-15). The third message warns against false worship (Rev. 14:9-12; idem, *Great Controversy*, pp. 453-54, 435-36). The "third angel's message" is really the marching orders of the Adventist movement and acts as a succinct summary of the movement's message when it says, "... the commandments of God, and the faith of Jesus."

gospel that began in earnest in the sixteenth-century Reformation.

For the Adventist, his movement is a "movement of destiny" (Froom). He sees it as destined to climax in what is called, in apocalyptic imagery, the "loud cry" (Rev. 14:7, 9; 18:1-2). This loud cry is viewed as a climactic gospel proclamation attended by the outpouring of the Holy Spirit in "latter-rain" power. All will have forced upon them a decision for or against Christ. After such a confrontation, the Lord will come again.

Notwithstanding the correctness or otherwise of this claim, it is nothing short of astounding. The Adventist believes that his movement and no other movement is God's chosen "remnant," especially commissioned by God to give the message of the gospel and so usher in the return of Christ.

At this point an evangelical churchman must pause and confess his shame. In so many of our "investigations" into Adventism this astounding conviction has received little or no elucidation. We have so often given the impression that Adventists are concerned about anything but the gospel and that the movement is characterized by a sectarian majoring on minors in matters of theology. We must apologize to Adventists for this terrible oversight. Let it be understood once and for all: any critique of Adventism which hopes to penetrate to the heart of the movement must come to grips with its concept of the gospel and its biblical and theological support for that concept. To fail here is to be wide of the (Adventist) mark.

From its own literature, we must now substantiate the existence of the Advent movement's astounding claim. We begin with Mrs. White: "The message of Christ's righteousness is to sound from one end of the earth to the other. ... This is the glory of God, which closes the work of the third angel."[19] The need of Adventists is to "become exponents of the efficacy of the blood of Christ, by which our own sins have been forgiven. Only thus can we reach the higher classes."[20] The "third angel's message" (i.e., the gospel of justification by faith)[21] is that which Adventists should be

---

19. Ellen G. White, *Testimonies for the Church*, 6:19. Statement written in 1890.

20. Ibid., p. 82. Statement written in 1890.

21. "Several have written to me, inquiring if the message of justification by faith is the third angel's message, and I have answered, 'It is the third angel's message in verity'"

preaching:

> When the third angel's message is preached as it should be, power attends its proclamation, and it becomes an abiding influence. It must be attended with divine power, or it will accomplish nothing. ...
>
> The sacrifice of Christ is sufficient; he made a whole, efficacious offering to God; and human effort without the merit of Christ, is worthless.[22]

Some of Mrs. White's statements concerning the center of Adventist preaching are so fine that we shall take the liberty of indulging ourselves somewhat:

> Ministers are to present Christ in His fulness both in the churches and in new fields. ... It is Satan's studied purpose to keep souls from believing in Christ as their only hope. ...[23]

> Of all professing Christians, Seventh-day Adventists should be foremost in uplifting Christ before the world. ... the great center of attraction, Christ Jesus, must not be left out.[24]

> The message of the gospel of His grace was to be given to the church in clear and distinct lines, that the world should no longer say that Seventh-day Adventists talk the law, the law, but do not teach or believe Christ.[25]

> The sacrifice of Christ as an atonement for sin is the great truth around which all other truths cluster. ... This is to be the foundation of every discourse given by our ministers.[26]

> Let the science of salvation be the burden of every sermon. ... Bring nothing into your preaching to supplement Christ. ...[27]

> Lift up Jesus, you that teach the people, lift Him up in sermon, in song, in prayer. Let all your powers be directed to pointing souls, confused, bewildered, lost, to "the Lamb of God."[28]

(Ellen G. White, *Review and Herald*, 1 Apr. 1890; quoted in idem, *Selected Messages*, 1:372).

22. Ellen G. White, "The Righteousness of Christ," *Review and Herald*, 19 Aug. 1890.

23. Ellen G. White, *Gospel Workers*, p. 162.

24. Ibid., p. 156.

25. Ellen G. White, *Testimonies to Ministers and Gospel Workers*, p. 92. Statement written in 1890's.

26. White, *Gospel Workers*, p. 315.

27. Ibid., p. 160.

28. Ibid.

In language too clear to be misunderstood Mrs. White says, "Justification by faith and the righteousness of Christ are the themes to be presented to a perishing world."[29] One subject will swallow up every other:

> If through the grace of Christ his people will become new bottles, he will fill them with the new wine. God will give additional light, and old truths will be recovered, and replaced in the frame-work of truth; and wherever the laborers go, they will triumph. As Christ's ambassadors, they are to search the Scriptures, to seek for the truths that have been hidden beneath the rubbish of error. And every ray of light received is to be communicated to others. One interest will prevail, one subject will swallow up every other— Christ our righteousness.[30]

In *Selected Messages*, Book One, Mrs. White makes it clear that the message of Adventism is the gospel of justification by faith alone:

> Some of our brethren have expressed fears that we shall dwell too much upon the subject of justification by faith, but I hope and pray that none will be needlessly alarmed; for there is no danger in presenting this doctrine as it is set forth in the Scriptures. If there had not been a remissness in the past to properly instruct the people of God, there would not now be a necessity of calling special attention to it. ... The exceeding great and precious promises given us in the Holy Scriptures have been lost sight of to a great extent, just as the enemy of all righteousness designed that they should be. He has cast his own dark shadow between us and our God, that we may not see the true character of God. The Lord has proclaimed Himself to be "merciful and gracious, long-suffering, and abundant in goodness and truth."
>
> Several have written to me, inquiring if the message of justification by faith is the third angel's message, and I have answered, "It is the third angel's message in verity."[31]

Many other citations could be given from the writings of Mrs. White.[32] However, the above are more than sufficient to show that,

---

29. Ellen G. White, Letter 24, 1892.

30. Ellen G. White, "Be Zealous and Repent," *Review and Herald Extra*, 23 Dec. 1890.

31. White, *Selected Messages*, 1:372. Statement written in 1890.

32. E.g.: Ellen G. White, *Review and Herald*, 29 Nov. 1892; idem, *Testimonies to Ministers*, pp. 91-2 (Here Mrs. White says, "This [the mesage of justification by faith] is the message that God commanded to be given to the world."); idem, *Gospel Workers*, p. 161.

as far as she was concerned, the mission of Adventism, *par excellence*, is the proclamation of the gospel of righteousness by faith with unprecedented power and glory.

Next we shall return to the late Dr. Froom. In his book, *Movement of Destiny*, he corroborates the testimony of Mrs. White. In a chapter entitled "Our Bounden Mission and Commission," Dr. Froom writes as follows:

Christ-centered Preaching Marks Radiant Climax

1. *Every Doctrine Actualized in Christ.*—Our Mission involves Christ-centered preaching and teaching in the grand finale, to a degree hitherto unattained. Especially is this to be as we come to the radiant climax of our witness. ...

2. *To Be Foremost Preachers of Christ.*—We are today to become, in all the world, the foremost preachers of *Christ in all His fullness.* ... A host will respond.

We are called upon to place every aspect of our message in its true Christ-centered setting. ... Then to preach doctrine will always be to preach Christ.[33]

In a section entitled "Christ's Righteousness Our Indispensable Passport," Dr. Froom shows every bit as clearly as does Mrs. White what the heartthrob of the final message to men will be.[34] This glorious provision is to constitute the inner heartthrob, and it is for the world as well as for the church. It will be Christ's perfect life and Christ's perfect commandment-keeping. Dr. Froom says unequivocally that righteousness by faith "in its larger inclusive scope will constitute the core and essence of it all." It will be remembered, he continues, that the everlasting gospel is the essence and the dynamic of our final message to mankind. This constitutes the shape of things that are to come.[35]

Using copious citations from two of the most illustrious exponents of Adventism, we have shown the precise nature of the special commission that Adventists claim has been vouchsafed to them by God. In viewing the sources of this movement, one cannot escape the conclusion that it is a movement bound up with the gospel. And of course, this means that it stands or falls with the

---

33. Froom, *Movement of Destiny*, p. 649. Emphasis in original.
34. Ibid., pp. 650-51.
35. Ibid., p. 660.

legitimacy or otherwise of its gospel.

To conclude this chapter, we make three further comments:

1. In order to treat the Seventh-day Adventist according to the criterion of the movement itself, his well-known negative stance toward Rome has to be seen in the light of the above perspective.[36] Although the Adventist has often conveyed the idea that he is opposed to the mere abuses and excesses of Rome, in actual fact his truest position is from the standpoint of his divine calling to re-emphasize and consummate the gospel of the Reformers.

2. The oftentimes puzzling attitude of the Adventist toward Protestants is also to be seen in the same light. He has often given the impression that he is separate on the basis of matters of the law only. But this is not his deepest problem. He is committed to the conviction that, in general, Protestants have apostatized from the Reformation gospel and its implications and have thereby begun a landslide toward the papal curia. The Adventist believes that he is called by God to prevent such a landslide as much as possible. He must, as a member of the faithful "remnant,"[37] demonstrate to the Protestant world (and indeed to all) the deepest significance of the gospel and the glory of God. This is what motivates his stance toward Rome[38] as well as his stance toward Protestants.

3. We must deal with still another aspect of the Adventist consciousness. A knowledge of this aspect will undoubtedly place the above-mentioned stupendous claim into more correct perspective

---

36. This aspect of Adventism was humorously expressed when a little boy on a TV quiz program was asked the question, "What is a Seventh-day Adventist?" He replied, "A Seventh-day Adventist does not eat meat, and he hates Catholics!"

37. The "remnant" idea is a major motif in Adventist thinking, but it is by no means without diversity of interpretation. For further information on the "remnant" motif in Adventism, see Seventh-day Adventist Bible Commentary, 7:812-15, and the numerous "Ellen G. White Comments" references on p. 815; Robert H. Pierson, We Still Believe, pp. 171f.; Kenneth H. Wood, "The Role of the Seventh-day Adventist Church in the End Time," pp. 26f., in Biblical Research Committee of the General Conference, ed., North American Bible Conference, 1974; Froom, Movement of Destiny, the entire book.

38. For examples from more modern writers expressing the anti-Roman Catholic stance of Seventh-day Adventism, see Seventh-day Adventist Bible Commentary, esp. vols. 4 and 7. In volume 4 there is a commentary on the book of Daniel (see esp. pp. 819-47). In volume 7 there is a history of the interpretation of the Apocalypse (see pp. 118-30) and comments on Rev. 13 (see pp. 816-24). Froom, Prophetic Faith of Our Fathers, is important as an indication of the essentially unchanging position of the movement concerning Roman

and substantiate our thesis that the movement is one which is peculiarly bound up with the gospel of the Reformation.

For almost ninety years Adventists have been preoccupied with the gospel in a way that can only be called remarkable. Adventism has had to face a very serious question which cannot but have been raised within the movement—namely, Why has the "loud cry" not taken place? Why has the Lord not come? One answer is that some forty odd years after the inception of the movement, the Lord graciously sought to give the church a knowledge of the gospel with unprecedented clarity. Unfortunately and tragically, she by and large rejected that gracious donation. Since the year 1888, in one way or another and to a greater or lesser degree, the Adventist Church has grappled with precisely what took place regarding her response to the message of 1888. The year 1888 has truly been a "thorn in the flesh" for the Adventist Church. For some ninety years she has been struggling with her relationship to the gospel of the Reformation. No understanding of the movement would scrape beyond the surface if it failed to take this factor into consideration. (See appendix at the end of this chapter for a synopsis of Adventism's struggle with the gospel.)

Therefore, alongside the stupendous claim of the Adventist Church must be placed the fact that she has recognized her failure to carry out the special commission of the Lord. Hence, there is widespread "beating of the breast."

Whatever else the struggle over the church's response to the message of 1888 shows us, it does substantiate our claim that Adventism has been preoccupied with the gospel and with its approach to the gospel for some ninety years of its 133-year existence. We believe that this aspect of the movement justifies in no small way a treatment of the validity of the Adventist claim to maintain the gospel of the Reformation. Perhaps such a critique may even be able to assist the movement in self-clarification.

———————————

Catholicism. Froom contends that Adventism stands in the historicist line of interpreters down the ages and that Protestants with their futurism, etc., have departed from that tradition. Rome is the antichrist. See also George McCready Price, *The Greatest of the Prophets*. For Price's comments on Dan. 7 and 8, see pp. 133-216. When Adventism speaks of Rome as the antichrist, this does not refer simply or even primarily to the "abominable excesses" of Rome. The reference is to the doctrinal heart of Rome—namely, her view of the gospel.

Appendix

1888: A Thorn in the Church's Flesh

All Adventists who know their own history will acknowledge that in the year 1888 a revival took place in the church. Two Adventist ministers, Elders E. J. Waggoner and A. T. Jones, became obsessed with the doctrine of justification by faith alone and sought to present it with no small degree of fervor to the church.

A reaction took place—the precise nature of which has never been determined in the Adventist movement. It appears that although some, including Mrs. White,[39] accepted the message, most rejected it.

Things had more or less settled down within the church until 1924, when an ex-President of the General Conference, Elder A. G. Daniells, resurrected the whole question of the 1888 message and the church's response to it. In a publication entitled *Christ Our Righteousness*, Daniells left no doubt that he believed the message had been rejected. Here are his words:

> How sad, how deeply regrettable, it is that this message of right-eousness in Christ should, at the time of its coming, have met with opposition on the part of earnest, well-meaning men in the cause of God! The message has never been received, nor proclaimed, nor given free course as it should have been in order to convey to the church the measureless blessings that were wrapped within it. The seriousness of exerting such an influence is indicated through the reproofs that were given. These words of reproof and admonition should receive most thoughtful consideration at this time. ...[40]

Daniells proceeds to record some scathing indictments from Mrs. White against those who rejected the message at that time.[41] She

---

39. It appears that 1888 had a decisive influence on Mrs. White's appreciation of justifica-tion by faith. The doctrine receives much more extensive and explicit treatment by her after 1888 than before.

40. Arthur G. Daniells, *Christ Our Righteousness*, p. 47. Cf. esp. pp. 40f.

41. Ibid., pp. 47-52.

does not mince words. Mrs. White accuses the church of preaching the law "until we are as dry as the hills of Gilboa, that had neither dew nor rain." What is needed, she goes on to say, is not trust in our own merits, but in the merits of Jesus of Nazareth.[42]

Naturally, such a presentation was destined to bring unrest. There was a demand, not least from the laity, for an explanation. Was Daniells correct, or did the church really embrace the gospel at that time? Was this a clue as to why the "loud cry" had not taken place? Should the church repent, or should she silence those making such unfounded accusations?

A series of defenses took place. In 1947, Lewis H. Christian published *The Fruitage of Spiritual Gifts*. In this book he declared that although the session in 1888 had been tense, opposition had all but vanished a few years later in a virtually unanimous acceptance of the message of righteousness by faith.

In 1948 another defense appeared. Bruno William Steinweg submitted a thesis to the Seventh-day Adventist Theological Seminary entitled "Developments in the Teaching of Justification and Righteousness by Faith in the Seventh-day Adventist Church after 1900." Steinweg's thesis declared that the church had not rejected the gospel donation from the Lord in 1888. Were not Waggoner and Jones popular convention speakers after 1888? How could it be possible that they had been rejected if this was the case?

Another notable defense to appear was a book entitled *Captains of the Host* (1949), written by Adventist historian, A.W. Spalding. This book acknowledged that a crucial confrontation did take place in 1888 and that there was a divided reception. In the final analysis, however, 1888 was a victory for the church and not a defeat. The message of 1888 was not rejected.

A significant turn of events took place when two missionaries, R. J. Wieland and D. K. Short, presented a manuscript in 1950 to the General Conference of the Seventh-day Adventist Church. The manuscript was called *1888 Re-examined*. In no uncertain terms Wieland and Short asserted that the church had rejected the message that the Lord sought to give her at Minneapolis in 1888. She was guilty and should beat her breast and cry to the Lord for

---

42. See Ellen G. White, *Review and Herald*, 13 Aug. 1889; 11 Mar. 1890.

forgiveness. There must be corporate repentance. This author had the privilege of spending some time with Mr. Wieland in his home in Chula Vista, California, and it was obvious that, after almost thirty years, he still maintained this deep conviction.

Unprecedented conflict arose in the wake of this presentation by Wieland and Short—a conflict which lasted with a great degree of intensity for more than a decade. This intense dialogue concerning the response of the church to the message of 1888 was gathered up by A.L. Hudson in a publication entitled *A Warning and Its Reception*. Among other things, this contains Wieland and Short's thesis and its rejection by the leadership of the church.

Not long after, in 1962, another publication, *By Faith Alone* — originally a thesis submitted to the Seventh-day Adventist Theological Seminary by Norval F. Pease—appeared in defense of the church. There was ample evidence to show that the light of the gospel was not extinct in the Adventist history before 1900. But Mr. Wieland was not impressed. To him there was a vast difference between *some* gospel and the gospel in "loud-cry" dimensions.

Still the church was protected—this time by the publication in 1966 of a book by A.V. Olson called *Through Crisis to Victory: 1888-1901*. The title speaks for itself. Though there was a crisis, by 1901 victory had been gained for the church. Olson concluded his book by observing that wherever he traveled throughout the world among Adventists, he found a ready acceptance of the doctrine of righteousness by faith. Adventists believed it and indeed cherished it. Those who would suggest that the church rejected it were simply not correct.

A theological heavyweight then appeared on the scene to finally lay the question of 1888 to rest. In 1971, Dr. LeRoy Edwin Froom published his influential *Movement of Destiny*. In a characteristic manner he defended the church and delivered an offensive against those who would seek to cast her in a bad light over the 1888 message. Dr. Froom called for an explicit confession of wrong from all who would assert otherwise. But notwithstanding the magnitude and method of approach, the good doctor failed to lay the ghost of 1888 to rest.

In 1973 there was the first official acknowledgment of guilt since A.G. Daniells first resurrected the 1888 question. Reporting on the annual fall conference, the General Conference leaders admitted that 1888 occupied considerable attention at their gathering:

One question, therefore, has overshadowed all other subjects at this 1973 Annual Council: What has happened to the message and experience that by 1892 had brought the beginning of earth's final message of warning and appeal?[43]

The admissions made in answer to this question must have brought deep gratification to the heart of Mr. Wieland:

As a body the Church still is in the Laodicean condition as set forth by the true Witness in Rev. 3:14-19. Therefore, in attempting to find the specific present causes for failure and delay, the council has noted three main factors:

1. Leaders and people have not fully accepted as a personal message Christ's analysis and appeal to the Laodiceans (Rev. 3:14-22).

2. Leaders and people are in some ways disobedient to divine directives, both in personal experience and in the conduct of the church's commission.

3. Leaders and people have not yet finished the church's task.[44]

While it is obvious that the above would bring gratification to the heart of a man who has been calling his church to corporate repentance for over twenty years, the fact remains that repentance has not been forthcoming. Even the above statement is couched in language designed to soften the beating on the church's breast.

Still that is not the end of the drama. Agitation over the church's approach to the gospel of justification by faith alone reached an unprecedented high in May of 1976. A group of leaders and theologians met at Palmdale, California, to see if some agreement could be gained on the meaning of the gospel of righteousness by faith. The center of attention was the Professor of Systematic Theology at Avondale College, New South Wales, Australia—Dr. Desmond Ford. A statement was prepared (known as the Palmdale statement) which included a section on the meaning of righteousness by faith. There was also a section dealing with the 1888 era. The portion on 1888 is worth quoting in full:

---

43. *Review and Herald*, 6 Dec. 1973. The significance of the reference to 1892 is that Mrs. White said in that year that the "loud cry" was here in the 1888 message if accepted (White, *Selected Messages*, 1: 363).
44. Ibid.

In reviewing the history of the 1888 era, we are led to the conclusion that it was a time of unparalleled opportunity for the Seventh-day Adventist Church. The Lord actually gave His people the "beginning" of the latter rain and the loud cry in "the revelation of the righteousness of Christ, the sin-pardoning Redeemer." The attitudes and spirit manifested by too many at that time made it necessary for God to withdraw this special blessing.

While nothing is gained by disputing over the actual number of those who accepted or rejected this blessing in 1888, we recognize that those who then heard the message of righteousness by faith were divided in their response. It is clear that the fullness of the marvellous blessing God wanted to bestow upon the church was not received at that time nor subsequently. In the light of these facts of history, our special concern now must be to remove every barrier that holds back the promised power, and by repentance, faith, revival, and reformation clear the way so that the Lord can do His special work for us and through us. We recognize that a primary responsibility in this respect lies with the leadership of the church.[45]

If this is the case, what about the prior charges made against those who have asserted that the church has been culpable and needs to repent, especially the charges contained in such an influential publication as Froom's *Movement of Destiny*? This has not been overlooked. In *The Ministry* magazine of August, 1976, the following "apology" appeared:

We sincerely regret that that element of the book *Movement of Destiny* which so publicly demanded an "explicit confession" from those who saw the 1888 experience in a different light from that in which the leadership of the church viewed it was allowed to slip into print. We would recommend that this element be removed from any future printings of the book.

The drama of the church's response to 1888 is not yet finished. Many would like to see it finished. There are those within the church and on the edge of the church that have pledged themselves to keep agitating until corporate repentance is a reality and the gospel of justification by faith alone comes from the lips of Adventists in "latter-rain" power. Then, it is believed, the Lord will come, and 1888 may finally be laid to rest, or rather be given its full resurrection status.

---

45. "Christ Our Righteousness," *Review and Herald*, 27 May 1976, p. 6.

2

The Heart
of the Reformation

One of the truly amazing aspects of the sixteenth-century Reformation was the *unity* of the Reformers on the article of justification
by faith alone. They disagreed on many things, but on this point
they were unanimous. In his great classic, *The Doctrine of Justification*, James Buchanan writes, "Few things in the history of the
Church are more remarkable than the entire unanimity of the
Reformers on the subject of a sinner's Justification before God."[1]
Buchanan goes on to say that this remarkable fact can be ascribed
"to a copious effusion of the Holy Spirit, awakening everywhere
deep convictions of sin, and enlightening men's minds in the
knowledge of Christ as an all-sufficient Saviour."[2] James Orr
likewise refuses to regard it as accidental that at various centers
the minds of men simultaneously awoke to a clear apprehension of
the great doctrine of justification.[3] Here, then, lies the first great
trait of the Reformation—*unanimity on the doctrine of justification
by faith alone*—a unanimity which, as much as anything else in
the Reformation, bears testimony "to a copious effusion of the Holy

---

1. James Buchanan, *The Doctrine of Justification*, p. 165.
2. Ibid., p. 166.
3. James Orr, *The Progress of Dogma*, p. 244.

Spirit."

We have seen that the Reformers were united on the doctrine of justification. But what was the nature of this unity? The answer is clear: the Reformers were united on the *meaning* of justification and on its *place* in the life and teaching of the church.

The Place of Justification

We shall first look at the *place* of justification in the thinking of the Reformers. One could hardly state this more effectively than did John Bugenhagen, the friend of William Tyndale: "We have only one doctrine: Christ is our righteousness."[4] Unqualified centrality! Centrality in all doctrine and life! That was the place of the doctrine of justification in the Reformation.

Luther saw justification in the whole Bible. It is "the proposition of primary importance."[5] Indeed, said Luther, "Christ wants us to concentrate our attention on this chief doctrine, our justification before God, in order that we may believe in Him."[6] It is "the cardinal doctrine,"[7] "the true and chief article of Christian doctrine."[8] Many more citations could be given from Martin Luther to show that justification was his theological Katherine von Bora.[9]

Calvin took the same position. For him, justification "is the first

---

4. Quoted in J. F. Mozley, *William Tyndale,* p. 54.

5. Martin Luther, "Lectures on Genesis" (1535), *Luther's Works*, 4:400.

6. Martin Luther, "Sermons on the Gospel of St. John" (1530), *Luther's Works*, 23:109.

7. Ibid., p. 207.

8. Martin Luther, "Preface to the Acts of the Apostles," *Luther's Works*, 35:363.

9. See Martin Luther, "Lectures on Galatians, 1535," *Luther's Works*, 26:3, 176. Concerning the place of justification, Luther said, "Amisso articulo Justificationis, simul amissa est tota doctrina Christiana." The Smalcald Articles (1536) state: "On this article rests all that we teach and practice against the pope, the devil and the world" (pt. 2, art. 1, in Theodore G. Tappert, ed. and trans., *The Book of Concord*, p. 292). For the "chief-article" nature of justification, see Martin Luther, *D. Martin Luthers Werke: Kritische Gesammtausgabe*, 38:115. See also Tappert, *Book of Concord*, p. 292; Luther, *Luther's Works*, 12:27; 21:59; 22:145; 26:9; 54:340. For the intimate connection between justification and all doctrine, see idem, *D. Martin Luthers Werke*, 46:20f. An example of the foundational nature of this doctrine in Luther's thought is given by Dr. T. F. Torrance in "Eschatology," *"Scottish Journal of Theology" Occasional Papers*, no. 2, p. 41, with reference to the relation of *imputatio* to Luther's eschatological perspective. The believer possesses a *real* righteousness and one that is not yet realized.

and keenest subject of controversy."[10] Some have been puzzled by the fact that, in his great *Institutes of the Christian Religion*, Calvin dealt with regeneration *before* justification. But the purpose of this is to highlight justification: "... if we rightly acknowledge this truth [regeneration], it will be all the clearer how man is justified by faith alone and by nothing further than forgiveness."[11] After commencing with the preoccupation of Rome (regeneration), Calvin proceeded to spell out with ruthless clarity the preoccupation of the Reformation (justification). For him, this article was the foundation of all true piety and doctrine.

Here, then, is the second great characteristic of the Reformation: the overwhelming *centrality* of justification before God by faith alone.

The Meaning of Justification

Now let us look at the third significant characteristic of the Reformation. What did the Reformers *mean* by justification?

When we examine Luther on this aspect, we must read his "Lectures on Galatians" and not his "Lectures on Romans." In the "Romans" Luther was still the evangelical Catholic; in the "Galatians" he was the Protestant Reformer.[12] In his "Lectures on Galatians"[13] Luther declared:

> But the doctrine of Justification is this, that we are pronounced righteous and are saved solely by faith in Christ, and without works. ... it immediately follows that we are pronounced righteous neither through monasticism nor through vows nor through masses nor through any other works. ...

10. John Calvin, "Calvin: Theological Treatises," in *Library of Christian Classics*, 22:234, Calvin writing to Sadoleto. Cf. John Calvin, *Institutes of the Christian Religion*, tr. Ford Lewis Battles, bk. 3, chap. 11, sec. 1; bk. 3, chap. 15, sec. 7.

11. Calvin, *Institutes*, tr. Battles, bk. 3, chap. 3, sec. 1.

12. Luther's "Lectures on Romans" must not be confused with his later and famous "Preface to the Epistle to the Romans." His lectures on Romans were given in 1515-16. Luther's so-called "tower experience" probably occurred in the fall of 1518. It was this cataclysmic event that gave him his great insight into the gospel of justification by faith alone. Thus, his "Lectures on Romans" is a reflection of Luther as a young evangelical Catholic rather than of the Protestant Reformer. Luther's "Lectures on Galatians" was first published in 1535 and represents the clearest expression of his views on justification.

13. Luther, "Lectures on Galatians, 1535," *Luther's Works*, 26-27. See also idem, *D. Martin Luthers Werke*, 40 I:355, 33.

Justification means *to be pronounced righteous*. Further, Luther
said:

> The article of justification, which is our only protection, not only
> against all the powers and plottings of men but also against the
> gates of hell, is this: by faith alone (*sola fide*) in Christ, without
> works, are we declared just (*pronuntiari iustos*) and saved.[14]

When Luther says "by faith alone... *in Christ*," he does not, of
course, mean Christ *in us*. The righteousness which is the basis of
our acceptance with God lies *outside* the believer. Justifying righteousness is a righteousness which is *foreign* to the believer, an
alien righteousness. Luther is explicit:

> [A Christian] is righteous and holy by an alien or foreign
> holiness—I call it this for the sake of instruction—that is, he is
> righteous by the mercy and grace of God. This mercy and grace is
> not something human; it is not some sort of disposition or quality in
> the heart. It is a divine blessing, given us through the true knowl-
> edge of the Gospel, when we know or believe that our sin has been
> forgiven through the grace and merit of Christ. ... Is not this
> righteousness an alien righteousness? It consists completely in the
> indulgence of another and is a pure gift of God, who shows mercy
> and favor for Christ's sake. ... Therefore a Christian is not for-
> mally righteous; he is not righteous according to substance or
> quality—I use these words for instruction's sake. He is righteous
> according to his relation to something: namely, only in respect to
> divine grace and the free forgiveness of sins, which comes to those
> who acknowledge their sin and believe that God is gracious and
> forgiving for Christ's sake, who was delivered for our sins (Rom.
> 4:25) and is believed in by us.[15]

For Luther, justification means *to be pronounced righteous on the
grounds of a righteousness which is outside the believer, in Jesus
Christ*.

Calvin was likeminded on the meaning of justification. Justification is the divine pronouncement that the believing sinner is just
because of the merits of Jesus Christ.[16] Once again, the two significant points are (1) *to pronounce righteous* (2) *on the grounds of*

---

14. Ewald M. Plass, comp., *What Luther Says*, 2:701.
15. Ibid., pp. 710-11.
16. Calvin, *Institutes*, tr. Battles, bk. 3, chap. 11, secs. 5-12.

the merits of Christ.

Both these aspects were contrary to the teaching of the Church of Rome. Later, in the Council of Trent, she was to spell out her opposing view of justification—that it does not mean to merely *pronounce* righteous but to actually *make* righteous: "...the alone formal cause is the justice of God, not that whereby he himself is just, but that *whereby he maketh us just.* ..."[17] This *making just* of Rome means making the believer to be just *in himself.* Whereas the Reformers held that Jesus Christ alone is the justifying righteousness of the believer, Rome taught that the believer is given a righteous heart and that it is this which makes him acceptable to God:

> ...so if they [Christians] were not born again in Christ, they never would be justified; *seeing that in that new birth, there is bestowed upon them*, through the merit of his passion, *the grace whereby they are made just.*[18]

Here lies the whole conflict of the Reformation. Whereas Rome taught that justification means to *make* the believer just by the work of inner renewal in his heart, the Reformers taught that justification is the *declaration* by God that the believer is just on the grounds of the righteousness of Christ alone, which is outside the believer.

We wish to make one further point before we leave the Reformation meaning of justification. For the Reformers, justification has two sides—a *negative* side and a *positive* side. The negative side is the acquittal of the believing sinner on the grounds of the dying of Jesus Christ. Therefore, justification was sometimes spoken of simply as forgiveness.[19] So it is that justification is having the curse removed from us because of the death of Jesus, who bore the curse on our behalf.[20] Justification, however, is not only that God sees us in the light of Jesus' death for our sins. It also has a positive

---

17. The Council of Trent, sess. 6, Jan. 13, 1547, chap. 7 (cause 5 of justification); quoted in John H. Leith, ed., *Creeds of the Churches*, p. 412. Emphasis supplied.

18. Council of Trent, sess. 6, chap. 3; quoted in Leith, *Creeds of the Churches*, p. 409. Emphases supplied.

19. See Calvin, *Institutes*, tr. Battles, bk. 3, chap. 11, secs. 2, 11. This side of justification was stressed particularly to ward off the notion that justification also includes regeneration.

20. Ibid., bk. 3, chap. 11, secs. 3-4, 11.

aspect. Justification is unto life. God credits Jesus' perfect fulfillment of the law to the believer. He not only stands forgiven, but he stands clothed with the law-keeping righteousness of Jesus Christ at God's right hand. In Christ, the believer has met the requirement of the law. In Christ, he possesses by faith a perfect law-keeping life.[21]

Grace Alone

The meaning of justification in the Reformers will help us to grasp what they meant by justification by *grace alone*. What the Reformers meant by God's grace was that it is His sheer mercy and goodness revealed in sending His Son into Palestine to live and to die in order that we might have a perfect righteousness before God. Thus, the grace of God always refers to God and never to what is in the believer's heart. Calvin put it beautifully: grace is "God of his mere gratuitous goodness... [being] pleased to embrace the sinner."[22] It is "unmerited kindness,"[23] "the mercy and free love of the heavenly Father towards us."[24]

Paul Tillich correctly observed that the Reformers' (particularly Luther's) idea of grace was the real breakthrough in the sixteenth century. Tillich tells us that for Luther, grace means to be accepted in spite of being unacceptable. Luther explains grace in his famous "Preface to the Epistle to the Romans":[25] "The difference between 'grace' and 'gift' is this: *Grace,* in the proper sense of the term, denotes *God's favor and good will towards us*, which He cherishes in Himself. ..."

Of course, the Council of Trent saw things quite differently. For Trent, grace is something that is *bestowed* upon Christians which *makes* them just.[26] Grace is something which is voluntarily *re-*

---

21. Ibid., bk. 3, chap. 17, sec. 8; bk. 2, chap. 17, sec. 5.
22. Calvin, *Institutes*, tr. Henry Beveridge, bk. 3, chap. 11, sec. 16.
23. Ibid., bk. 3, chap. 13, sec. 1.
24. Ibid., bk. 3, chap. 14, sec. 17.
25. The reader should again be reminded that this "Preface" is not the same work as Luther's "Lectures on Romans."
26. See Council of Trent, sess. 6, chap. 3; quoted in Leith, *Creeds of the Churches*, p. 409.

ceived.[27] On this point Canon 11 of the Council of Trent is clear and forthright:

> If any one says that men are justified either by the sole imputation of the justice [righteousness] of Christ or by the sole remission of sins, to the exclusion of the grace and *the charity which is poured forth in their hearts by the Holy Ghost,* and remains in them, or also that the grace by which we are justified is only the good will of God, let him be anathema.[28]

As we have seen, Luther and Calvin understood saving grace as being God's action in Jesus Christ for the believing sinner. The idea that grace is the assistance God gives the believer in keeping the law was shunned by the Reformers as being the Roman Catholic teaching which only detracts from the glory of Christ and disturbs consciences. No, saving grace is God's saving action in Jesus Christ. *Christ* is the righteousness by which we are justified, and *Christ* is the expression of the grace of the Father.

Christ Alone

Luther and Calvin did not simply stress *Christ alone* over against the Roman Catholic emphasis on works-righteousness. The Reformers also stressed Christ alone over against all—be they Roman Catholics or Protestants[29]—who would point to the inside of the believer as the *place* where justifying righteousness dwells. Christ alone means literally Christ *alone,* and not the believer. And for that matter, it does not even mean any other member of the Trinity!

We must explain ourselves. For Luther and Calvin, Christ alone

---

27. See Council of Trent, sess. 6, chap. 7; quoted in Leith, *Creeds of the Churches,* pp. 411-12.

28. Council of Trent, sess. 6, can. 11; quoted in Leith, *Creeds of the Churches,* p. 421. Emphasis in original.

29. E.g., Osiander. See Tappert, *Book of Concord,* pp. 539f. Cf. "In opposition to the teaching of the Reformers, which holds justification to be a declaratory act, a pronouncing righteous, Osiander demands a positive, real justification instead of a negative one. He regards justification as an *actus physicus,* by which man is in reality *made* righteous, i.e. the righteousness of Christ is imparted to him. Accordingly he looks at justification and sanctification as being identical" (Henry Eyster Jacobs, ed., *The Lutheran Cyclopedia,* art. "Osiander, Andrew").

meant Jesus Christ the God-man alone, and *not the life of the
believer — even if it be admitted that such a life is caused by grace.*
No, justifying righteousness is to be found only in the one unique
God-man.

But we must state this still another way. For the Reformers,
Christ alone meant Jesus Christ the *God-man,* and *not Christ's
indwelling the believer by the Holy Spirit.* Some sought to subtly
modify the Reformation stress on justification. They were happy
with all such nice-sounding phrases as "justification by Christ
alone" and "Jesus Christ is the grace of God," so long as they could
make them refer not only to the God-man at the right hand of the
Father, but to the indwelling of Christ by the Holy Spirit in the
believer. However, to make this shift from the God-man to the
indwelling Christ is to abandon the Reformation doctrine of justification rather than to honor and perpetuate it.

To begin with, this shift makes the *believer* the place of justification, whereas for the Reformers the place of justification was Jesus
Christ in Palestine and at the right hand of the Father. Next, this
shift from the risen Christ at God's side to the indwelling of Christ
by the Spirit confuses Jesus Christ with the Holy Spirit. It attributes to the Spirit what in actual fact belongs to Christ alone. The
Reformers knew that Christ can only be said to indwell the believer by the Holy Spirit. The God-man, Jesus, is in heaven. But
there is still a further point: To make justifying righteousness
consist in the indwelling Christ is to have an *unfinished work* as
the basis of acceptance with God, rather than the *finished work* of
the God-man, Jesus of Nazareth. It is not difficult to see how an
unfinished basis of acceptance would detract from the glory of the
perfection-requiring God and unsettle tender consciences! Dr.
Buchanan says:

> Whereas, if we are justified on the grounds of the work of the Holy
> Spirit *in* us, we are called to rest on a work, which, so far from being
> finished and accepted, is not even begun in the case of any unre-
> newed sinner; and which, when it is begun in the case of a believer,
> is incipient only... marred and defiled by remaining sin... and
> never perfected in this life.[30]

---

30. Buchanan, *Doctrine of Justification*, p. 402.

The champions of the Reformation were clear. Justification by Christ alone means to be declared just on the grounds of the doing and dying of Jesus Christ alone. Luther declares:

> Therefore a man can with confidence boast in Christ and say: "Mine are Christ's living, doing, and speaking, his suffering and dying, mine as much as if I had lived, done, spoken, suffered, and died as he did."[31]

This is faith in the *substitutionary* Christ and the *imputed* Christ, and not the indwelling Christ. Calvin, the giant of Geneva, is like-minded:

> For if righteousness consists in the observance of the law, who will deny that Christ merited favor for us when, by taking that burden upon himself, he reconciled us to God as if we had kept the law.[32]

The "as if" is the inevitable result of believing in the gospel of salvation by *substitution* and *imputation*. Justification is by Christ alone, apart from the believer, and is not to be confused with the renewing work of the Holy Spirit.[33]

Faith Alone

It should now be evident that anyone who invests faith with any merit and worth in itself simply does not understand the Reformer's view of justification. For Luther and Calvin, *faith alone (sola fide)* was an expression, not a qualification, of *grace alone* and *Christ alone*.[34] Christ, who effected *satisfaction* by His life and His death, also effects the *appropriation* of that satisfaction. The

---

31. Luther, *Luther's Works*, 31:297.

32. Calvin, *Institutes*, tr. Battles, bk. 2, chap. 17, sec. 5.

33. The Formula of Concord says: "... without any merit or worthiness on our part, and without any preceding, present, or subsequent works, by sheer grace, solely through the merit of the total obedience, the bitter passion, the death, and the resurrection of Christ our Lord, whose obedience is reckoned to us as righteousness" (art. 3, in Tappert, *Book of Concord*, pp. 540-41).

34. See Calvin, *Institutes*, bk. 3, chap. 1, sec. 1. See also Luther, who says: "But the Scriptures set before us a man who is not only bound, wretched, captive, sick and dead, but who, through the operation of Satan his Lord, adds to his other miseries that of blindness, so that he believes himself to be free, happy, possessed of liberty and ability, whole and alive ..." (Martin Luther, *The Bondage of the Will*, p. 162). "... but no one can give himself faith, and no more can he take away his own unbelief" (idem, *Luther's Works*, 35:371).

former (satisfaction) He effected by His life and death in Palestine, and the latter (appropriation) He effects by His dispensing of the Spirit from heaven.

Faith is only the *instrument* and the enshrinement in the salvation process. Calvin called it an "empty vessel." Faith has no intrinsic power. It does not save because of any worthy capacity in the one who exercises it. Said Calvin:

> The power of justifying, attached to faith, consists not in the worthiness of the act. Our justification depends solely on the mercy of God and the merit of Christ, which when faith apprehends it is said to justify.[35]
>
> For unless we come empty with the mouth of our soul open to implore the grace of Christ, we cannot receive Christ. ... For faith, although intrinsically it is of no dignity or value, justifies us by an appreciation of Christ, just as a vessel full of money constitutes a man rich.[36]

In calling faith "instrumental" or an "empty vessel," the Reformers wished to clearly distinguish between faith itself and the merits of Christ, which faith apprehends and holds. *Faith* and its *object* must be clearly distinguished at all times if God is to receive the glory due to His name and if the conscience of the believer is to be protected.

Righteousness by Faith

Along with Paul, the Reformers also spoke of the "righteousness of [or by] faith" in contradistinction to the righteousness which *accompanies* and *follows* faith. The righteousness of faith is the righteousness which faith apprehends—namely, the doing and dying of the God-man, Jesus Christ. It is the righteousness which is the *object* of faith, and not any quality *in, with,* or *after* faith.

As mentioned above, when faith is understood as an "instrument" or an "empty vessel," it does not confuse the righteousness of Christ with anything *in* faith. Thus, the Reformers spoke of the

---

35. Calvin, *Institutes*, bk. 3, chap. 18, sec. 8.
36. Ibid., bk. 3, chap. 11, sec. 7.

"righteousness of faith" to protect it from being confused with anything *with* or *after* faith.

The Reformers acknowledged that faith in the righteousness of Christ in heaven is never present *without* regeneration and renewal, and that good works follow as a consequence of faith. But the righteousness of faith is not, in whole or in part, that renewal which is present *with* faith. Neither is it that renewal which *follows* faith. The righteousness of faith is never to be confused with sanctification. It is not sanctification, nor does it include sanctification.

This clear distinction between the righteousness of faith and sanctification was the massive breakthrough made by Martin Luther. The medieval church had mingled the two types of righteousness. But when this synthesis was rent asunder in the mind of Luther, the Protestant Reformation was born. Luther called the righteousness of faith (i.e., the righteousness of Christ) a *passive* righteousness because we have it *while we do nothing for it.* He called the other righteousness (i.e., that which is the result of faith) an *active* righteousness because it is the diligent good works of the believer performed through the operation of the Holy Spirit. The passive righteousness is *perfect,* for it is Christ's righteousness; the active righteousness is *imperfect,* for it is the work of sinful men. The former righteousness is by faith alone; the latter righteousness is by good works engendered by faith. The former is *justification;* the latter is *sanctification.*[37]

Chemnitz offers another way of making the contrast. He speaks of (1) the righteousness of Christ, which is imputed to the believer, and (2) the righteousness of the law:

> For the righteousness of the Law is that a man does the things that are written in the Law; but the righteousness of faith is by believing to appropriate to oneself what Christ has done for us. Therefore the works by which the regenerate do those things which are written in the Law, either before or after their renewal, belong to the righteousness of the Law, though some in one way, others in another. ...
>
> ...the obedience of Christ is imputed to us for righteousness. That glory cannot be taken away from Christ and transferred to

---

37. See Martin Luther, "Two Kinds of Righteousness," *Luther's Works*, 31:297-306.

either our renewal or our obedience without blasphemy.[38]

> But the righteousness of faith is to believe that Christ the Mediator has satisfied the Law for us for righteousness to everyone who believes (Rom. 10:4).[39]

Likewise, the Formula of Concord is explicit. The Spirit works the righteousness of the law in us, but that is not our righteousness before God. It should not be "considered or set up as a part or cause of our righteousness [before God], or otherwise under any pretext, title, or name whatever."[40]

Sometimes curses are given with greater clarity than are blessings. The Formula of Concord is not easy to misunderstand when it says: "We must criticize, expose and reject ... [that] righteousness by faith before God consists of two pieces or parts, namely, the gracious forgiveness of sins and, as a second element, renewal or sanctification."[41]

In concluding our remarks on the righteousness of (or by) faith, it should be said that the clear distinction between the "righteousness of faith" and sanctification is the teaching of all the Reformers. To reject this distinction is to lapse back into the synthesis of medieval Catholicism and to repudiate the unanimous teaching of the fathers of the Reformation.

Perfectionism

The distinction between the two types of righteousness will make the final emphasis of the Reformation easier to understand. The Reformers contended that *the believer is righteous in this life only by faith*. In saying this, they were not denying either the necessity or the reality of sanctification in all true believers. Rather, they were asserting that in this life *sanctification is never good enough to stand in the judgment*. The believer must look *only* to the righteousness of faith (the righteousness of the God-man) for his

---

38. Martin Chemnitz, *Examination of the Council of Trent*, pt. 1, pp. 490-91. Cf. Rom. 10:4.
39. Ibid., p. 528.
40. Formula of Concord, art. 3 of "The Solid Declaration," in Tappert, *Book of Concord*, p. 549.
41. Ibid., pp. 547-48.

acceptance with God.

The inadequacy of sanctificational renewal was an integral part of Reformation teaching. Its corollary was the Reformers' steadfast gaze at the righteousness of faith—namely, the doing and dying of the God-man, Jesus of Nazareth. Though the believer fights against sin and seeks to be a faithful law-keeper, sin nevertheless remains until his dying day. Luther put it forcefully:

> Paul, good man that he was, longed to be without sin, but to it he was chained. I too, in common with many others, long to stand outside it, but this cannot be. We belch forth the vapours of sin; we fall into it, rise up again, buffet and torment ourselves night and day; but, since we are confined in this flesh, since we have to bear about with us everywhere this stinking sack, we cannot rid ourselves completely of it, or even knock it senseless. We make vigorous attempts to do so, but the old Adam retains his power until he is deposited in the grave. The Kingdom of God is a foreign country, so foreign that even the saints must pray: "Almighty God, I acknowledge my sin unto thee. Reckon not unto me my guiltiness, O Lord." There is no sinless Christian. If thou chancest upon such a man, he is no Christian, but an anti-Christ. Sin stands in the midst of the Kingdom of Christ, and wherever the Kingdom is, there is sin; for Christ has set sin in the House of David.[42]

We must beware of being holier than Paul and Luther and a host of other saints down through the ages! It was Rome who put herself in just such a position. In the Council of Trent she asserted:

> If any one denies, that, by the grace of our Lord Jesus Christ which is conferred in baptism, the guilt of original sin is remitted, *or says that the whole of that which has the true and proper nature of sin is not taken away* . . . let him be anathema.[43]

Perfectionism in this life is a major aspect of the gospel of the Church of Rome, just as the sinfulness of all good works is a major assertion of the Reformers. All who insist on perfection in the

---

42. Quoted in Karl Barth, *Romans*, p. 263. Cf. "Every good work of the saints while pilgrims in this world is sin" (Martin Luther, "Against Latomus," *Luther's Works*, 32:159).
43. Council of Trent, sess. 5, sec. 5; quoted in Leith, *Creeds of the Churches*, p. 407. Cf. the following statements from the Council of Trent: "If any one says that in every good work, the just man sins at least venially, or what is more intolerable, mortally, and hence merits eternal punishment, and that he is not damned for this reason only, because God does not impute those works unto damnation, let him be anathema" (p. 423). "If any one says, that the one justified sins when he performs good works . . . let him be anathema" (p. 424).

believer in this life, in whatever shape or form, reiterate the teaching of Rome and not that of the Reformers.

Calvin was no less dogmatic than Luther on the reality of sin in the justified. In the Geneva Confession are these words:

Remission of Sins Always Necessary for the Faithful

Finally, we acknowledge that this regeneration is so effected in us that, until we slough off this mortal body, there remains always in us much imperfection and infirmity, so that *we always remain poor and wretched sinners in the presence of God*. And, however much we ought day by day to increase and grow in God's righteousness, *there will never be plentitude or perfection while we live here.* Thus we always have need of the mercy of God to obtain the remission of our faults and offences. And so we ought always to look for righteousness in Jesus Christ and not at all in ourselves, and in Him be confident and assured, putting no faith in our works.[44]

Lest it be thought that the sinfulness of the believer is something the Reformers failed to see in relation to the sovereign Lordship of Christ, as if they were denying His power to deliver them from it, we need to turn to Luther's "Lectures on Galatians." Here he shows that remaining sin is used positively by God in the salvation of the believer:

Thus there is great comfort for the faithful in this teaching of Paul's, because they know that they have partly flesh and partly Spirit, but in such a way that the Spirit rules and the flesh is subordinate, that righteousness is supreme and sin is a servant. Otherwise someone who is not aware of this will be completely overwhelmed by a spirit of sadness and will despair. But for someone who knows this doctrine and uses it properly even evil will have to cooperate for good. For when his flesh impels him to sin, he is aroused and incited to seek forgiveness of sins through Christ and to embrace the righteousness of faith, which he would otherwise not have regarded as so important or yearned for with such intensity. And so it is very beneficial if we sometimes become aware of the evil of our nature and our flesh, because in this way we are aroused and stirred up to have faith and to call upon Christ. Through such an opportunity a Christian becomes a skillful arti-

---

44. The Geneva Confession; quoted in Lewis W. Spitz, ed., *The Protestant Reformation*, p. 117. Emphases supplied.

san and a wonderful creator, who can make joy out of sadness, comfort out of terror, righteousness out of sin, and life out of death, when he restrains his flesh for this purpose, brings it into submission, and subjects it to the Spirit. Those who become aware of the desires of their flesh should not immediately despair of their salvation on that account. It is all right for them to be aware of it, provided that they do not assent to it; it is all right for anger or sexual desire to be aroused in them, provided that they do not capitulate to it; it is all right for sin to stir them up, provided that they do not gratify it. In fact, the godlier one is, the more aware he is of this conflict. This is the source of the complaint of the saints in the Psalms and throughout Scripture. The hermits, monks, sophists, and all the work-righteous know nothing whatever about this conflict.[45]

We must not think that Luther and Calvin thought lightly of the demands of the law in the life of the Christian. Both Reformers said that the believer keeps the law but that he does not do so to perfection. The practical implications of this perspective were that *justification on the grounds of the doing and dying of Christ was kept central* in the preaching and teaching of the Reformation, and *the hope of eternal blessedness was based firmly on justification and not sanctification.*

---

45. Luther, "Lectures on Galatians, 1535," *Luther's Works*, 27:74-5.

Part II

Adventism and the Reformation before 1950

Introduction to Part II

We have tried to understand the Adventist as he understands himself, and the resulting picture is quite different from many portrayals of Adventism from outside the movement. The Adventist sees himself as especially chosen by God to bring the arrested Reformation of the sixteenth century to its God-designed close. Such a task will involve a proclamation of the gospel in "latter-rain" power such as is not possible with any other religious body.

We then turned our attention to the heart of the Reformation to refresh our understanding of the gospel of Luther and Calvin. The object was to give us a clear grasp of the norm by which we are to measure the way that Adventists have executed their task and made good their astonishing claim.

In Part II of this book we shall trace their execution of that task from the inception of the movement to the year 1950. As the 1950-1977 era is the main focus of this work, there will be no attempt to treat the earlier period exhaustively.

Two additional preliminary remarks: The desire of this author is to be a sympathetic investigator, for it is believed that such a one makes the best critic. Also, Adventism is being viewed as a dynamic movement, so final judgment will be reserved for the movement at the point of its most mature expression.

3

Off to an Inauspicious Start: 1844-1888

The founders of the Seventh-day Adventist Church must have been tough and determined characters. They were survivors of a great religious shipwreck. The spectacular Advent awakening movement of the 1840's,[1] sometimes called the Millerite movement, had run aground on the rocks of "The Great Disappointment" in the fall of 1844. Christ had not come as confidently predicted.

Although forever cured of the temptation to set definite time for the eschaton, these few survivors did not give up hope in the nearness of the advent. They retained much of the elaborate prophetic framework inherited from the Millerite movement, and to this was added the belief that the final judgment hour had arrived in the heavenly sanctuary, the teaching of the non-immortality of the soul, and the keeping of the seventh-day Sabbath. They believed that the finger of prophecy marked them as the last-day "remnant" (Rev. 12:17), called of God to preach the final gospel invitation to every nation and tribe on earth in preparation

---

1. In the summer of 1844 there were 50,000 confessing Adventists by the most conservative estimate.

for Christ's return (Rev. 14:6-14).

These pioneers of Seventh-day Adventism were like an army pitifully decimated. Most of their comrades and all of their leaders had fallen.[2] Not one notable religious figure graced their company. They had no churchman of rich religious heritage to lead them. They possessed no great theological erudition. Most of them were rather poor. And they were already separated from the mainstream of the Christian church. No one, looking on, would have given them much chance of success, especially with what could appear as a disastrous start. Apart from the charismatic influence of the young Ellen White, they might have called it quits. But her contribution inspired these survivors with an astonishing sense of destiny and world mission.

The question before us is straightforward. How did Seventh-day Adventists execute their task of preaching and teaching the "third angel's message" in the 1844-1888 period? Perhaps it is best to allow Adventists themselves to answer the question, for this author is by no means the first to examine the period.

One Adventist to summarize this era was Norval Pease. In his Masters dissertation at the Seventh-day Adventist Theological Seminary in 1945,[3] he examined the status of the doctrine of justification in the Adventist Church prior to 1888. He concluded that it was almost entirely absent. Pease writes: "The records of this period of four decades have not been found plentiful; and instances of mention of this particular doctrine are comparatively few."[4] He goes on to mention that a statement made by Mrs. White indicates that she and her husband had been alone for forty-five years in teaching this doctrine.[5] Mrs. White's statement receives endorsement from the early Adventist periodicals and books, which, says Pease, "reveal a famine of material in this field."[6] From August 15 to December 19, 1854, the masthead of the *Review and Herald* listed the "Leading Doctrines Taught by the *Review*," and

---

2. By 1849 there were only 100 Sabbatarian Adventists.
3. Norval F. Pease, "Justification and Righteousness by Faith in the Seventh-day Adventist Church before 1900."
4. Ibid., p. 28.
5. Ibid.
6. Ibid., p. 31.

this list "included absolutely no mention of justification, right-eousness, or any related topic."[7] Pease pauses in his fruitless search and observes:

> Thus far, the trend of the four decades ending in 1888 is evident. Up until the middle eighties the subject of justification and righteous-ness by faith was practically untouched in Seventh-day Adventist periodicals and books, aside from occasional references by James White.[8]

Pease records that this condition was aptly commented upon by Mrs. White in a camp-meeting address at Rome, New York, June 17, 1889. On this occasion she stated:

> I have had the question asked, what do you think of this light which these men [A. T. Jones and E. J. Waggoner] are presenting? Why, I have been presenting it to you for the last forty-five years, — the matchless charms of Christ. This is what I have been trying to present before your minds. When Brother Waggoner brought out these ideas at Minneapolis, it was the first clear teaching on this subject from any human lips I had heard, excepting the conversa-tion between myself and my husband.[9]

The judgment of this Adventist pastor and historian is not to be questioned. In the 1844-1888 period there was almost a total failure on the part of Adventists to acknowledge the fundamental tenet of the Reformation. Except for a few cursory comments of J. H. Waggoner, the almost universal position was that *acceptable right-eousness before God is found through obeying the law with the aid of the Spirit of God.* This was an essentially semi-Pelagian view of righteousness by faith (i.e., that acceptance with God is the result of the cooperation of human and divine effort). In other words, *justification* on the grounds of the imputed righteousness of Christ was subordinated to *sanctification* of the believer by inner renewal. There was no advance toward the position of the Reformers until that which came in 1888 under the leadership of A. T. Jones and E. J. Waggoner.

We shall now attempt to support this contention from the litera-

---

7. Ibid. Cf. p. 33.
8. Ibid., p. 35.
9. Ibid.

ture of the period, which reveals how justification was subordinated in a Roman Catholic fashion by the Adventist teachers of the
first four decades. There were four major characteristics of the
Seventh-day Adventist approach to the gospel which lead us to this
conclusion:

1. Justification was subordinated to sanctification in that justification was seen to be *only for the sins of the past*. J. H.
Waggoner,[10] James White,[11] and Uriah Smith[12] all expounded the
significance of Christ's work as being only for the sins of the past.
This relegation of the righteousness of Christ to the past was aided
by the fact that, in the first four decades, Adventist teaching on the
gospel of the Reformation gave almost no place to the *active* obedience (life) of Jesus Christ. The accent was always on the *death* of
Christ for the sins of the past.[13] If the life of Christ was mentioned,
it was only spoken of as exemplary.[14]

2. Justification is given the status of *mere* justification. It is not
as though this is said in so many words. Rather, it is the general
tendency of all the examined expositions of the period. There is an
overwhelming emphasis on the *law* and a correspondingly lesser

10. J.H. Waggoner, *Justification by Faith*.

11. "God's law... leads him [the sinner] to Christ, where justification for past offenses can
be found alone through faith in His blood. The law of God has no power to pardon past
offenses..." (James White, *Review and Herald*, 10 June 1852, p. 24).

12. In 1872, Uriah Smith published *A Declaration of the Fundamental Principles of the
Seventh-day Adventists*. Though he was the author, it did not bear his name since it was to
represent the whole of Adventism. Article 15 stated: "That, as all have violated the law of
God, and cannot of themselves render obedience to his just requirements, we are dependent on Christ, first, for justification from our past offenses, and, secondly, for grace whereby
to render acceptable obedience to his holy law in time to come."

13. See Uriah Smith, *The Sanctuary and the Twenty-three Hundred Days of Daniel VIII.
14*, pp. 245-47. From this it is apparent that Smith believed in Christ as our Substitute, but
he saw significance only in Jesus' death. We have found nothing where Smith suggests
that Christ was also our Substitute in holy obedience.

14. See James White, *The Redeemer and Redeemed; or, the Plan of Redemption through
Christ*, pp. 3-13. White says: "This is redemption in its first stage. It is deliverance from the
power of darkness, and a translation above the corruptions of this world into the kingdom
of Christ's abounding grace" (p. 8). "The death, resurrection, and the ascension of the Son
of God were events of great importance in the plan of human redemption; but with no one
of these is the plan finished. The Redeemer was to make two distinct advents to this world.
At the first, he lived our example, preached his own gospel, wrought miracles to confirm
his divine mission, died our sacrifice, rose from the dead for our justification, and ascended
to the Father's right hand to plead the cause of the repenting sinner" (p. 13). See also idem,
Life Incidents in Connection with the Great Advent Movement, p. 354; idem, *Bible Adventism; or Sermons on the Coming and Kingdom of Our Lord Jesus Christ*, pp. 196-97.

emphasis on the *gospel*. For a case in point, a book was published by Roswell F. Cottrell, entitled *The Bible Class: Lessons upon the Law of God, and the Faith of Jesus*. On the title page the words "Law of God" appear in large type, while the words "Faith of Jesus" appear in considerably smaller type. This might be excused as merely a blunder on the part of the typesetter. However, the book itself devotes the first fifty-nine pages to a discussion of the law, then ten pages to the faith of Jesus, or the gospel. The life of Jesus is spoken of only as exemplary. Cottrell was later to oppose the message of 1888.[15]

Because the overwhelming concern of the Adventists of this period was preparation for the coming of Christ and, in particular, the acquiring of a righteousness which would be good enough to see them through the "time of trouble," they stressed the imperative to such an extent that the indicative was diminished. Thus, their religion was *hagiocentric* (focused on the saint).

3. In the light of the above, it is not difficult to understand the emphasis that is unceasing in the time up to 1888—namely, that *acceptance in the last judgment is on the basis of the believer's sanctification* (and in particular, on inward grace).

J. H. Waggoner stated this strongly in his book, *Justification by Faith*. He was fighting antinomianism and Calvinism. For him, judgment on the basis of works was the deathblow to both antinomianism and the Calvinist doctrine of "eternal security." He saw judgment according to works as being the opposite of justification by faith.

For Uriah Smith, Christ forgives the past and provides grace and strength to enable us to obey in the future and thus obtain acceptance before God.[16]

---

15. See Robert J. Wieland and Donald K. Short, *1888 Re-examined*, p. 62.

16. "That the new birth comprises the entire change necessary to fit us for the Kingdom of God and consists of two parts: First, a moral change, wrought by conversion and a Christian life; secondly, a physical change at the second coming of Christ. ..." "That, as the natural or carnal heart is at enmity with God and his law, this enmity can be subdued only by a radical transformation of the affections, the exchange of unholy for holy principles; that this transformation follows repentance and faith, is the special work of the Holy Spirit, and constitutes regeneration or conversion" (Smith, *Declaration*, arts. 5, 14). We do not agree with L. E. Froom, who says that this *Declaration* was less representative than Smith averred (Froom, *Movement of Destiny*, p. 160).

According to the writers of this period, inner renewal or transformation may be spoken of as either the righteousness of Christ or
the righteousness of (or by) faith. It is the righteousness of Christ
because it is *His* work in the heart, and it is the righteousness of
faith because it springs from (is the result of) faith.[17]

In the early covenant theology of the Adventists, the new-
covenant work of the Mediator is minimized in the interest of
acquiring acceptable sanctification for the judgment.[18] The fault of
the old covenant lay not in the conditions enjoined on the people
nor in their promises to fulfill those conditions, but *in their inabil-
ity and failure to keep the law*. Hence, a new arrangement was
necessary. The grace of God is given—the law is written on the
heart in regeneration—and this enables the believer to keep the
law acceptably and stand in the judgment of God.[19] Thus, the
person freed from sin by faith in Jesus will enter the city of God as a
commandment-keeper.[20] So it is that *justification by law,* as G. I.
Butler explained it under this doctrinal scheme, is taken to mean
seeking acceptance with God on the grounds of one's own effort

---

17. So, in opposition to E. J. Waggoner and A. T. Jones, see Uriah Smith, "Our Righteousness," *Review and Herald*, 11 June 1889. See also idem, *Review and Herald*, 10 May 1892,
for Smith's view of the man of Rom. 7, which is the same as that taken by the Church of
Rome at the time of the Reformation. To Smith's credit it must be said that in early 1891 he
realized he had made a terrible mistake at Minneapolis, confessed his wrong, and pledged
himself to support the truth he had once spurned. But even then he apparently did not
realize its tremendous importance (see A. V. Olson, *Through Crisis to Victory: 1888-1901*,
pp. 92-103).

18. See John Nevins Andrews, *Sermon on the Two Covenants*; "M. H.," *The Two Laws, and
Two Covenants*.

19. J. N. Andrews in 1851 recognized that Christ "was 'made under the law', kept the
covenant which requires perfect obedience, then died for our transgressions, and be-
queathed to us his own inheritance" (John Nevins Andrews, *Thoughts on the Sabbath and
the Perpetuity of the Law of God*, p. 16). However, he apparently failed to see the significance of what he had written.

20. "By faith in the blood of Christ, we can be cleansed from sin—the cause of our sickness
can be removed, and by obeying the laws of health, we may have right to the tree of life.
But let all who have applied to the Physician of souls for a cure, be careful not to expose
their health again, by breaking the commandments of God. ... Faith is nothing more than
firm belief; but it is of so much importance in the plan of salvation, that the whole plan is
called 'the faith.' In this sense, the faith is not merely an act of the mind, the same as belief,
but it includes various requirements which are to be obeyed. [Acts 6:7; Rom. 1:5; 16:26;
2 Tim. 4:7; Rev. 14:12 quoted.] These passages show that... all that we are required to do in
order to be saved from sin belongs to the faith of Jesus. The person thus freed from sin by
the faith of Jesus, will enter the City of God as a commandment keeper the same as if he
had never sinned. Rev. 22.14" (Roswell F. Cottrell, *The Bible Class: Lessons upon the Law
of God, and the Faith of Jesus*, pp. 61-2).

without the aid of the Spirit of God, who has come to help the believer do that (keep the law) which those under the old dispensation could not do and which he (even now) could not do "in his own strength."[21] This teaching's striking affinity with Tridentine theology will not be missed.[22]

4. Another essential feature of the Tridentine scheme is *perfectionism*. Perfectionism was predominantly implicit in this period, but it becomes explicit in the following two periods to be examined. Perhaps time was needed for the logic of the theological position to become apparent. Yet it was beginning to surface even in the early decades of the movement. Though James and Ellen White had occasion to rebuke proponents of the perfectionism of the holiness movement,[23] statements with a decidedly perfectionistic flavor were not lacking from James White.[24] A corollary of his view that

---

21. "'Christ is become of no effect unto you, whosoever of you are justified by law; ye are fallen from grace.' This verse is often separated from its connection, and used as having a bearing upon our personal justification by faith for our transgressions of the moral law. ... No man can be saved by his good works alone. 'All have sinned, and come short of the glory of God.' We are weak and utterly helpless of ourselves, covered with pollution, and never can remove our guilt and uncleanness by present or future efforts of obedience. Indeed, we are utterly weak and helpless; and if our sins *have* been forgiven, we must have constant faith in and help from a crucified Saviour, constant access to his unfailing fountain of strength, in order to obtain any real help or accomplish anything whatever that will meet God's favor in the line of good works. ... Yet ... the apostle ... is not speaking of being justified through obedience to the *moral* law" (George I. Butler, *The Law in the Book of Galatians: Is It the Moral Law, or Does It Refer to that System of Laws Peculiarly Jewish?* pp.74-5). Butler's views as quoted by Olson, *Through Crisis to Victory*, pp. 45-6, 86-7, should be noted.

22. That is, from the Roman Catholic Council of Trent.

23. "We are pained to learn the condition of Bro. B., and to know that Satan is pushing him on to cause disaffection in the Indiana Conference under the pious guise of Christian holiness. Both you and ourselves fully believe that holiness of life is necessary to fit us for the inheritance of saints in light. We contend that this state must be reached in a Bible way. Christ prayed that his disciples might be sanctified through the truth, and the apostles preached of purifying our hearts by obeying the truth. The professed church of Christ is full of the spurious article, and one distinct feature of it is, the more one drinks into the spirit of popular sanctification, the less he prizes the present truth. Many of those who are the open opponents of God's Sabbath, the third angel's message, and the health reform, are among the sanctified ones. Some of them have reached the almost hopeless position that they cannot sin. These, of course, have no further use for the *Lord's Prayer*, which teaches us to pray that our sins may be forgiven, and but very little use for the Bible, as they profess to be led by the Spirit. ... We warn our brethren of the Indiana Conference and elsewhere. Our position has ever been that true sanctification, which will stand the test of the Judgment, is that which comes through obedience of the truth and of God" (James and Ellen G. White, "Bogus Sanctification," *Review and Herald*, 6 June 1878).

24. See James White, *Review and Herald*, 29 Jan. 1857.

the judgment had begun was his view that, following the close of
the judgment, there would be a period of time before the actual
return of Christ during which men must live without a Mediator.
As White considered this, he became convinced that "a consecration every way as complete as" that of the dying sinner was in-
adequate to see the saints through this "time of trouble." The
consecration of *life* was higher than that of the one who dies in the
Lord.[25]

It appears that Mrs. White did not share the same perspective as
her husband in some central aspects of religion. LeRoy Edwin
Froom has given a graphic illustration of how James White's
primary emphasis was upon the law, while Ellen White's emphasis
was on the gospel.[26] Also, James White made a distinction between
the preparation for death and that which is essential for translation without seeing death. But Ellen White asserted that the same
preparation which prepares one for death also prepares one for
translation, for just as no change is to be made in the character at
the second advent, so none is to be made at death or the resurrection.[27] There is some disagreement over Mrs. White's position on
perfectionism. Yet this writer does not think that one is forced to
read perfectionism in her work.[28]

If our understanding of Mrs. White is correct, then we have to
say that it is her emphasis which is the most encouraging up to the
General Conference of 1888. This much is clear from her writings:
in the time leading up to 1888 there was a growing awareness that
all was not well with the remnant church.[29] According to Mrs.

25. James White, ed., *Life Sketches of James White and Ellen G. White*, p. 431.

26. Froom, *Movement of Destiny*, pp. 182-86.

27. E. G. White, *Testimonies*, 5:466-67; idem, *The Adventist Home*, p. 16; idem, *In Heavenly Places*, p. 227.

28. Norman F. Douty, *Another Look at Seventh-day Adventism*, would not agree with my conclusion here, although Anthony A. Hoekema, *Four Major Cults*, would. Cf. the follow-ing Ellen G. White references: *Sanctified Life*, pp. 7, 81; *Acts of the Apostles*, pp. 560-61; *Steps to Christ*, p. 65, which speak *against* perfection; and *Steps to Christ*, p. 62; *Review and Herald*, 26 Feb. 1901; *Selected Messages*, 1:198, 373, which seem to speak *for* perfec-tion. However, Mrs. White's perfection may be seen in the light of her emphasis on gospel to which we have already referred. Cf. the following Ellen G. White references: *Review and Herald*, 8 Mar. 1906; 3 Sept. 1901; *Questions on Doctrine*, p. 684; *Selected Messages*, 1:396; 2:32-3. The last citation reads: "We are not to be anxious about what Christ and God think of us, but about what God thinks of Christ, our Substitute."

29. "The church has turned back from following Christ her Leader and is steadily retreat-

White, all the emphasis on the law without the gospel left the remnant caught in the grip of dry legalism:

> We have long desired and tried to obtain these blessings, but have not received them because we have cherished the idea that we would do something to make ourselves worthy of them. We have not looked away from ourselves, believing that Jesus is a living Saviour.[30]

The remnant community was ready for a more excellent way.

---

ing toward Egypt" (E. G. White, *Testimonies*, 5:217). Cf. "The facts concerning the real condition of the professed people of God, speak more loudly than their profession, and make it evident that some power has cut the cable that anchored them to the Eternal Rock, and that they are drifting away to sea, without chart or compass" (idem, *Review and Herald*, 24 July 1888).

30. From a morning talk to the ministers assembled at the General Conference, Battle Creek, Mich., Nov., 1883; pub. in E. G. White, *Gospel Workers* (1892 ed.), pp. 411-15, under the title, "Christ Our Righteousness." Also: "In Him is our hope, our justification, our righteousness. ... At this very time He is carrying on His work in our behalf, inviting us to come to Him in our helplessness, and be saved. We dishonor Him by our unbelief. ... My brethren, are you expecting that your merit will recommend you to the favor of God, thinking that you must be free from sin before you trust His power to save? If this is the struggle going on in your mind, I fear you will gain no strength, and will finally become discouraged" (pp. 412-13).

4

Attempted Breakthrough: 1888-1950

We have observed that 1844-1888 was a lean and hungry period as far as the doctrine of justification in Adventism was concerned. But this was not all. Some of the foundation truths of Christianity were as scarce as justification itself. As one reads the period, he is never quite sure whether the little remnant community is going to emerge as truly Christian or not!

The story may well have been grim indeed had it not been for the quite unexpected revival of 1888. At the 1888 General Conference Session in Minneapolis, the doctrine of justification by faith hit the Adventist Church with unexpected fury. It was as if the truest reason for the community's existence were calling a dried-up people back to life and renewed vision. E. J. Waggoner and A. T. Jones were the instruments of the doctrine, with considerable support being given by Mrs. White herself.

The Message of 1888

At the General Conference Session of 1888, E. J. Waggoner gave talks on the law and the gospel,[1] showing that the central message

---

1. *General Conference Daily Bulletin*, "Second Day's Proceedings," 19 Oct. 1888, p. 2.

of Galatians was justification by faith and that the law in Galatians was the *moral* law. His studies continued until Thursday,
October 25.[2] On October 17-25, while Waggoner was giving his
lectures, Mrs. White delivered six discourses at the morning devo-
tionals, speaking of the need to be connected with Christ.[3] Her
expositions gave a great deal of emphasis to justification by faith
alone—an emphasis almost entirely absent prior to the 1880's.[4]
She spoke of the truth of justification by faith as having been
rescued from "the companionship of error" and placed in its proper
framework—meaning the Seventh-day Adventist framework,
which stresses the law and the gospel.

On the morning before E. J. Waggoner concluded his series, the
tone of Mrs. White's talks changed. She declared, "I never was
more alarmed than at the present time."[5] The cause of such alarm
was the apathy and antagonism toward the message of justification by faith that was being given at the conference. Some had
become intolerant of Waggoner.[6] Mrs. White, however, endorsed
Dr. Waggoner's teaching on justification by faith alone:

> I see the beauty of truth in the presentation of the righteousness of
> Christ in relation to the law as the Doctor has placed it before us.
> ...That which has been presented harmonizes perfectly with the
> light which God has been pleased to give me during all the years of
> my experience. If our ministering brethren would accept the doc-
> trine which has been presented so clearly,—the righteousness of
> Christ in connection with the law—and I know they need to accept
> this, their prejudices would not have a controlling power, and the
> people would be fed with their portion of meat in due season.[7]

Since no official record of E. J. Waggoner's messages at the
conference was kept, there is some uncertainty about what he
actually presented. L. E. Froom says that Waggoner's ninety-six-

2. Waggoner's series on Galatians brought controversy. Note the comment: "The lectures
have tended to a more thorough investigation of the truth, and it is hoped that the unity of
the faith will be reached on this important question" (*General Conference Daily Bulletin*,
26 Oct. 1888, p. 3).

3. Ibid.

4. See Ellen G. White, "Advancing in Christian Experience," Ms. 8, 1888; pub. in Olson,
Through Crisis to Victory, pp. 260-69.

5. Ellen G. White, Ms. 9, 1888, p. 1.

6. See Ellen G. White, Ms. 15, 1888.

7. Ibid., p. 2.

page book, *Christ and His Righteousness*, reflects his messages at that time. But the book makes no mention of the real bone of contention—the law in Galatians and its relation to the gospel. In a manuscript on E. J. Waggoner which is soon to be published,[8] David McMahon is probably more correct when he argues that Waggoner's pre-Minneapolis publication on *The Gospel in Galatians* is nearer to what he actually presented at the conference.

Froom says that Waggoner's positions are set forth principally in his three books, *Christ and His Righteousness*, *The Gospel in Creation*, and *The Glad Tidings*. However, Froom's claim that there is "uniformity and continuity of teaching throughout the three books"[9] is open to question in the light of recent research. In the 1890's, Waggoner began to move toward pantheism, and this is reflected in *The Gospel in Creation* (1894) and in *The Glad Tidings* (1900).

The great light of 1888 was that no amount of mere human obedience can satisfy the divine law. Therefore, only One who is both God and man can satisfy the law on our behalf. His righteousness may be obtained by simple faith. This righteousness is not offered merely for the past, but for the present and the future as well. Here, certainly, was a new note in Adventism. A. T. Jones put it as follows:

> ...some accepted it [the message at Minneapolis in 1888] just as it was given, and were glad of the news that God had righteousness that would pass the judgment, and would stand accepted in His sight—a righteousness that is a good deal better than anything that people could manufacture by years and years of hard work. People had worn out their souls almost, trying to manufacture a sufficient degree of righteousness to stand through the time of trouble, and meet the Saviour in peace when He comes; but they had not accomplished it. These were so glad to find out that God had manufactured a robe of righteousness and offered it as a free gift to every one that would take it, that would answer now, and in the time of the plagues, and in the time of judgment, and to all

---

8. David McMahon, *E. J. Waggoner: The Myth and the Man*.

9. Froom, *Movement of Destiny*, pp. 200-201. Cf. pp. 188-217. An examination of these books themselves will show that Froom is overstating his case when he says they all reflect in "documentary record" fashion what Waggoner said in 1888. It appears that at times Froom acted more in the character of an apologist and wishful thinker than that of an objective historian.

eternity, that they received it gladly just as God gave it, and heartily thanked the Lord for it.[10]

The thought that the believer has no part in producing the robe of righteousness, but has only to accept it by faith, ran counter to the semi-Pelagianism of the day and could scarcely fail to provoke a reaction.

However, while there was an advance, Jones and Waggoner in 1888 still looked upon justification as being, at least in part, a work of subjective transformation. They saw it as making the sinner righteous.[11] No clear distinction was made between imputed and imparted righteousness.[12]

As we have already seen, the great light of 1888 was that Christ was our Substitute in holy living. But Jones and Waggoner did not clarify the Pauline and Reformation insight as to how this justifying righteousness remains outside the believer. The door was left open to see this substitution in moral and ontological terms instead of legal and judicial terms. Waggoner and Jones soon lost their way. Even as early as 1891, Waggoner had come to the conclusion that what is done in heaven has no bearing on the sin problem at all. What is done in the sinner is what counts.[13] Waggoner followed these ideas right into pantheism.[14]

---

10. *General Conference Daily Bulletin*, 1893, p. 243. For further illustrations of the position of A. T. Jones, cf. Alonzo T. Jones, *The Present Truth*, 11 Feb. 1892, pp. 42-4. Cf. also idem, *The Revelation of God*, passim.

11. See. E. J. Waggoner, *Christ and His Righteousness*, pp. 29-32.

12. "Who could ask for more? Christ, in whom dwelleth all the fullness of the Godhead bodily, may dwell in our hearts, so that we may be filled with all the fullness of God. ... All the power that Christ had dwelling in Him by nature, we may have dwelling in us by grace, for He freely bestows it upon us" (ibid., pp. 31-2).

13. See E. J. Waggoner, "The Blotting Out of Sin," *Review and Herald*, 30 Sept. 1902, p. 8. Further examples of Waggoner's position are as follows: "He [Christ] shows its [the law's] righteousness by fulfilling, or doing, what it demands, not simply for us, but in us. ... the fact that the righteousness of the law could be attained in no other way by us than by the crucifixion and resurrection and life of Christ in us, shows the infinite greatness and holiness of the law" (idem, *The Glad Tidings*, p. 96). ". . . He [Christ] becomes our substitute . . . literally taking our place, not instead of us, but coming into us, and living our life in us and for us, it necessarily follows that the same law must be in our hearts [that was in Christ's heart] . . ." (p. 171). Cf. p. 169. See further: ". . . His name is 'God with us;' so to believe on His name means simply to believe that He dwells personally in every man, — in all flesh. We do not make it so by believing it; it is so, whether we believe it or not; we simply accept the fact, which all nature reveals to us" (pp. 80-81).

14. See Froom, *Movement of Destiny*, pp. 349-56. For instances of pantheistic theology in Waggoner, see E. J. Waggoner, *The Gospel in Creation*, pp. 66, 98-9, 112; idem, *Glad*

The problem of the 1888 renewal was twofold. First, although Waggoner and Jones moved in the direction of the Reformation in stressing the necessity of the doing and dying of the God-man in order to stand in the judgment, they did not possess enough light to see this in a completely Reformational *Christ alone* perspective. Second, the message met with more opposition than positive response. This meant that Waggoner and Jones missed out on a *corporate* investigation into truth—an investigation which might have preserved them from pantheism and set the Adventist community solidly in the path of the Reformation gospel.

We may sum up the whole period in general, and the 1888 period in particular, with the following words of Mrs. White:

> ...justification by faith is...the third angel's message in verity....
> As yet, we certainly have not seen the light that answers to this description.[15]

> We have only the glimmerings of the rays of the light that is yet to come to us. We are not making the most of the light which the Lord has already given us, and thus we fail to receive the increased light; we do not walk in light already shed upon us.[16]

The Aftermath of the 1888 Crisis

Notwithstanding the opposition to justification by faith at the Minneapolis conference, Waggoner, Jones, and Mrs. White traveled throughout the land after 1888, preaching the theme of the righteousness of Christ. Mrs. White did not spare the leaders her strong indictments for their antagonism,[17] even after she moved to Australia in 1891.[18] Some repented of their opposition; others retained it.

Tidings, pp. 80-81, 96, 169, 171. In 1891, Waggoner rejected entirely any idea of justification by faith being a legal transaction that takes place in heaven. Cf. idem, *Confession of Faith*, pp. 10-15.

15. Ellen G. White, *Review and Herald*, 1 Apr. 1890.

16. Ibid., 3 June 1890.

17. See E. G. White, *Testimonies to Ministers*, pp. 76, 79-80, 89-98.

18. Mrs. White was requested by the church leaders to return to the U.S.A. in 1896, but she said she would not because they were still in darkness. Cf. ibid., pp. 393, 396.

The period between 1901 (when the church was reorganized for more effective missionary outreach) and the early 1920's was a time of settling down and extending the work.[19] This settling down was largely due to the pantheism crisis which the Adventist Church experienced in the early years of this century. The brilliant doctor, J. H. Kellogg, with the support of A. T. Jones and E. J. Waggoner, sought to get the church to espouse an extreme concept of the indwelling of Christ in His "temple"—a view which amounted to a pantheism. The great preparation for the day of the Lord became the cleansing of the temple of the human heart—an approach which only pushed to the extreme the internalistic notion of justification which Waggoner had come to hold after 1888.

An Adventist, Robert Haddock, made the point that after the 1905 crisis the church reverted to a pre-1888 conservatism.[20] This is probably an accurate assessment of the 1888-1950 period in its entirety–a fact witnessed to by the "apologies" for the church concerning her response to the 1888 message. Nevertheless, the 1888 revival of the whole matter of righteousness by faith deeply affected the Adventist consciousness from that time on.

Froom saw the 1888 struggle largely in terms of a conflict between Adventist "distinctives" and the "eternal verities" of the Christian church. In the early period (1844-1888) Adventism began to recapitulate to some extent the history of the Christian church. Cut off from the main Christian stream, the Adventists of that time were unsettled on some of the great Christian truths— principally the Trinity, the deity of Christ, the sinless human nature of Christ,[21] and His finished atonement on the cross. Froom saw 1888 as a great step forward in that it led Adventism to be fully

---

19. My impressions from Mrs. White's writings during this period are that she more or less resigned herself to the idea that the church would continue to be around for some time. She wrote *The Desire of Ages* from Australia in 1898, and *Prophets and Kings* and *The Ministry of Healing* between 1901 and 1915, the year of her death. It was not that she stopped calling the church to ever higher standards. She continued to do that always and exerted not a little influence on the movement in this regard. However, one gets the impression that the rejection of the 1888 light was a greatly retarding factor in the movement's realization of what it believed to be its divinely given mission.

20. See Robert Haddock, "A History of the Doctrine of the Sanctuary in the Advent Movement: 1800-1905," p. 372. Cf. pp. 239-70.

21. Adventists have never doubted the sinlessness of Christ's life, but they have often taught that He inherited "sinful flesh."

settled on the doctrines of the Trinity and the full deity of Christ. However, he admitted that the revival did not complete the consolidation of what he called the "eternal verities." (One gets the idea that he felt it was his contribution to help Adventism become settled on the sinless human nature of Christ and His finished atonement on the cross. Agitation on these points did not come until the 1950's, however, and so we must defer discussion of this matter until later.)

It is not hard to understand why the church would "dig in" after the pantheism crisis of 1905, especially since those who attempted to introduce a new emphasis in 1888 were found to be advocating the pantheistic heresy. Further progress had to await the second half of this century, for evidence indicates that the Adventist community did not make any significant theological progress until the 1950's. From 1905 to the 1920's only W. W. Prescott revealed any creative thinking concerning the gospel. And, apart from some good insights here and there, he could not lead the movement on to greener theological pastures.

As we shall see, there was an attempt to infuse life into Adventism through the influence of the holiness movement. But this was to retard rather than forward the realization of the Adventist aim—namely, to further the work of the Protestant Reformation.

The Doctrine of Justification Up to 1950

In the 1888-1950 period Adventists were not unanimous on their definition of justification. There were those, for example, who defined justification in the Roman Catholic sense of *to make righteous*.[22] In a tract published in the mid-1890's, E. J. Waggoner seems to have accepted this unequivocal Roman definition.[23] And despite the fact that he encountered opposition to his Roman views,[24] he retained this understanding of justification. Moreover,

---

22. E.g., E. J. Waggoner, *Christ and His Righteousness*, p. 61. However, on page 63 Waggoner has a more Protestant tone: "...this forgiveness consists simply in the declaration of His [Christ's] righteousness...."
23. E. J. Waggoner, *The Power of Forgiveness*. Cf. idem. *The Present Truth*, 20 Oct. 1892, p. 323.
24. See E. J. Waggoner, *The Present Truth*, 23 Apr. 1896, p. 259.

Waggoner's internalistic emphasis intensified, as may be seen from his works already referred to.[25]

It is difficult to understand how Froom could have given his approval to these writings of Waggoner.[26] Froom said that Waggoner was always sound on "righteousness by faith." Either Froom "whitewashed" Waggoner, or he himself could not tell the difference between the Protestant and Roman Catholic positions on the meaning of justification.[27]

Among others who took the non-Protestant position that to justify means to make righteous were H. A. St. John,[28] Charles T. Everson,[29] A. G. Daniells,[30] A. W. Spalding,[31] and Bruno Steinweg.[32] The major emphasis in Adventism, however, has been the quite Protestant understanding of the meaning of justifica-

---

25. See n. 9 above.

26. See Froom, *Movement of Destiny*, pp. 526, 530.

27. A.V. Olson reveals that Froom was not the only one who took a most favorable attitude to the pantheistic works of Waggoner: "About a month after writing the lines just quoted, Elder Daniells wrote another letter to W. C. White, dated May 12, 1902, and referred again to the same situation as follows: 'I am deeply convinced that something ought to be done to place a flood of light in the homes of the people. I know of no better book to do this, outside of the Bible, than Brother Waggoner's book.' The book to which Elder Daniells alluded was *The Everlasting Covenant*, by J. H. Waggoner" (Olson, *Through Crisis to Victory*, p. 231). Olson wrongly ascribes *The Everlasting Covenant* to J. H. Waggoner. It was written instead by his son, E. J. Waggoner. The point is that *The Everlasting Covenant* contains both pantheism and an outright Roman Catholic view of salvation. One wonders why Daniells, Froom, and Olson did not know this. Was it that they thought this was Protestant doctrine?

28. ". . . How can unrighteous men become righteous? Well, the answer is plain. Christ is the Sun of Righteousness. He can and will write the law in the hearts of all truly penitent sinners. Through his Spirit the love of God is shed abroad in the heart, the carnal mind taken away, and the spiritual mind substituted. Thus the sinner receives the righteousness of Christ as a free gift" (H. A. St. John, *The Sun of Righteousness*, p.76).

29. Charles T. Everson, "Saved by Grace," in *Typical Evangelistic Sermons*. Recommended by the General Conference of Seventh-day Adventists. Currently available in tract form.

30. "'Righteousness by faith' is not a *theory*. People may hold a theory about it, and at the same time be 'ignorant of God's righteousness. . . .' 'Righteousness by faith' is a transaction, *an experience*. It is a submitting unto 'the righteousness of God.' It is a change of standing before God and His law. It is a regeneration, a new birth. Without this change there can be no hope for the sinner, for he will remain under the condemnation of God's changeless, holy law . . ." (Daniells, *Christ Our Righteousness*, p. 21). Emphases in original. In other places Daniells says that justification is "to declare" righteous and is by imputation. However, like Augustine and the early Luther, he confounds justification and regeneration and thereby militates against the realization of the Adventist mission.

31. "Justification . . . is an experience, not an argument. It is the new birth" (Arthur W. Spalding, *Origin and History of Seventh-day Adventists*, 2:282).

32. Bruno William Steinweg, "Developments in the Teaching of Justification and Righteousness by Faith in the Seventh-day Adventist Church after 1900," pp. 22-3, 46, 68.

tion.[33] W. H. Branson,[34] Norval Pease,[35] and a host of others agree that to justify means to declare righteous. Notwithstanding the exceptions, the movement has followed Luther and Calvin here.

We have seen that, in the Reformers, justification was given the status of being the central article around which all other articles are gathered, or, in the words of Calvin, "the hinge on which all true religion turns." We have also seen that in the 1844-1888 era this feature of Reformation theology was not honored. What of 1888-1950? It must be said that in this period *justification is generally subordinated to sanctification* in a Roman Catholic fashion. We shall make two points concerning this:

1. Justification is subordinated in that it is seen as *only for past sins*.

M. C. Wilcox, following the tradition of pre-1888, says unequivocally that "justification... always has reference to the past."[36] This essentially Wesleyan emphasis is not difficult to understand when the Wesleyan background of the movement is kept in mind, but we have to be critical of such an emphasis in light of Adventism's claim to further the work of the Reformation.[37]

Steinweg says of C. P. Bollman that he wrote frequently on the theme of justification by faith.[38] But although Bollman differentiated between justification and sanctification, he relegated justification to the beginning of the Christian experience.

Edwin Keck Slade in *The Way of Life* is a corrective influence. He speaks of justification as being for the past, present, and future.[39]

2. In harmony with the thinking of the early Adventists of 1844-1888, justification is subordinated as being *mere* or *only*.

33. E.g., Meade MacGuire, *The Life of Victory*, p. 23.
34. W. H. Branson, *How Men Are Saved*, pp. 37-45.
35. Pease, *By Faith Alone*, pp. 56-9.
36. M. C. Wilcox, *Justification, Regeneration, Sanctification*, p. 3. Cf. "...justification...is forgiveness of past sins only..." (p. 13). Cf. also idem, *Review and Herald*, 20 Mar. 1919, p. 3.
37. While writing this section, a flyer entitled *Quick Look at Seventh-day Adventists* (1976) came into my hands. It states: "Their work is to continue the task begun in Reformation times, to help reillumine principles tarnished or forgotten during Christianity's long and tortuous history."
38. Steinweg, "Developments in Justification and Righteousness by Faith," p. 25.
39. Edwin Keck Slade, *The Way of Life*, pp. 71, 73.

Norval Pease refers to "mere justification," showing this clear subordination in his thinking.[40]

Steinweg's manuscript[41] closely follows that of Pease, which was written a few years earlier. Interestingly enough, Steinweg also speaks of *mere* justification and goes on to say that righteousness by faith, in Adventist thinking, has meant justification *and* sanctification.

That justification between 1888 and 1950 is treated as *mere* may be seen from the fact that *regeneration and sanctification are seen as the higher stage in the salvation process*.

Norval Pease has said that the Adventist contribution has been to give a greater emphasis on sanctification than on justification.[42] If Pease meant by this that Adventists have given to sanctification the priority *over* justification, then his point is irrefutable; but whether this constitutes a real *contribution* to the Christian world remains to be seen.

M. C. Wilcox put the matter so baldly as to merit quoting:

> If justification is precious, regeneration is much more so. The one is forgiveness of past sins only, the other includes all of that, and also the change of that nature which caused us to sin.[43]

W. H. Branson in *How Men Are Saved* is no more tactful.[44] And Steinweg quotes M. L. Andreasen as saying that the "keeping power of God" is the "greater power" when compared with justification.[45] Andreasen says further that the need (in the 1930's) is sanctification, that "we might by faith gain not *only* forgiveness, but that keeping power of God that will enable us... to go and sin no more."[46]

This era does not break with the previous period in that *acceptance in the final judgment is said to be on the basis of the inward*

40. Pease, "Justification and Righteousness by Faith," p. 1.

41. Steinweg, "Developments in Justification and Righteousness by Faith."

42. "If the Adventist teaching of this doctrine is unique in any particular, it is in the emphasis on *righteousness* ...following the transaction of *justification* by faith" (Pease, *By Faith Alone*, p. 207). Emphases in original.

43. Wilcox, *Justification, Regeneration, Sanctification*, p. 13.

44. Branson, *How Men Are Saved*, p. 47.

45. Steinweg, "Developments in Justification and Righteousness by Faith," pp. 58-9.

46. Ibid., p. 59. Emphasis supplied.

grace of sanctification. With this emphasis, the superiority of sanctification in the salvation process is guaranteed.

Earlier we observed that, as far back as 1886, Uriah Smith saw justification as being for past offenses only, and taught the need of grace to render acceptable obedience to God's law in time to come.[47] In 1889, Smith makes it plain that he does not think of the believer as keeping the law in his own strength. This is really the role of the Christ within, the One who has come to change our nature. Christ pardons for the past and helps the believer to arrive at perfect conformity to the law, by which he can stand at last in the judgment.[48] It is encouraging that Mrs. White found occasion to pour scorn on Smith's statement.[49]

G. I. Butler had the same view as Smith;[50] and, notwithstanding Mrs. White's response to Smith, A. V. Olson in *Through Crisis to Victory* cites the Butler statement approvingly to show that Butler really did believe in righteousness by faith.[51]

E. J. Waggoner after 1891, while emphasizing the active and passive obedience of Christ, stressed that Christ performs this in the heart of the believer.

Hence, alongside the note from the Reformation, there is also a strong Roman Catholic emphasis. This Tridentine emphasis is taken up in 1950 by W. H. Branson, who speaks of those who comply with the requirement of the law by the power of the indwelling Christ.[52] If—and such is the case—this imparted righteousness is believed to be that upon which the believer depends for his acceptance in the last judgment, it is not difficult to see how sanctification becomes the all-absorbing passion.

The Reformation gospel was the gospel of the righteousness of Christ being put to the believer's account. While it was acknowledged that sanctification is received as the inseparable companion gift of justification, the Reformers saw the justified man as being

47. See chap. 3, nn. 12-13.
48. Uriah Smith, *Review and Herald*, 11 June 1889.
49. See Ellen G. White sermon, June 17, 1889, Ms. 5. Smith later defended his statement in a *Review and Herald* editorial of July 2, 1889.
50. George I. Butler, *Review and Herald*, 23 Sept. 1884.
51. Olson, *Through Crisis to Victory*, pp. 45-6. Cf. p. 47.
52. W. H. Branson, *Drama of the Ages*, p. 308.

fully righteous *only in Christ* and not, at any time, in himself. Adventism has thought otherwise. *Perfectionism* has been a recurring theme. Insofar as this is true, the *simul justus et peccator* (at the same time righteous and a sinner) of the Reformation has not been echoed.

Pease is somewhat embarrassed by the presence of perfectionism and sees it as not having been the majority view.[53] This is open to question, however. And as we shall see later, it appears that the perfectionistic doctrine has become the official position of the *Review and Herald* publishing section of the church.

The perfectionistic element within Adventism has a positive and a negative aspect. Positively, it springs from the correct insight — as far as the Reformation is concerned — that if one is to stand in the judgment, nothing less than *perfect* righteousness will do. Insofar as Adventism has grasped this, it has honored an aspect of Reformation theology which many Protestants have neglected. Negatively, however, Adventists have failed to appreciate the Reformation *answer* to the need for perfect righteousness. Instead of looking to the Christ at the right hand of God, as did the Reformers, Adventists have looked to themselves — aided of course by the indwelling Spirit, or the *Christ within* — to perform such righteousness.

In the period of the 1920's there arose a "victorious-life" emphasis within Adventism. The way this emphasis was expressed is indistinguishable from the evangelical "holiness movement." In fact, much of Adventist literature was openly indebted to authors from evangelicalism, as Wieland and Short have shown.[54] Implicit in the holiness theology is perfectionism. According to the holiness movement, perfection comes through a mighty infilling of the believer by God, *above* and *beyond* that experienced by believers who are *merely* justified. Crass Pelagianism is softened to a more refined semi-Pelagianism in the style of Trent. Emphasis is put upon the *Christ within*, who lives out His perfect life in and through the believer.[55]

Some within Adventism equated the "victorious life" of evangel-

---

53. Pease, *By Faith Alone*, pp. 207-8.
54. See A. L. Hudson, ed., *A Warning and Its Reception*, pp. 224-31.
55. Hence: "The victorious life is attained only through an indwelling Christ. He alone can

ical pietism with righteousness by faith and gave clear articulation to the implicit perfectionism of the movement.[56] Norval Pease
fails to see how this perfectionistic tendency is inimical to the
Adventist claim to continue the gospel of the Reformation and,
even if that is waived, to the claim that their message is something
which neither Roman Catholics nor evangelical Protestants
possess.[57]

A. G. Daniells[58] in *Christ Our Righteousness* gives a Protestant
statement on justification[59] but then speaks of its content in
sanctificational terms reminiscent of Trent.[60] He says that the
experience of justification is to receive "His [Christ's] righteousness and His life," and this is a "wondrous transformation," a
"great transaction by which sinners are changed to saints."[61]
Righteousness by faith, we are told, includes victory over sin
"through the indwelling Christ."[62]

Many other works could be cited to illustrate the influence of the
implicitly perfectionistic holiness movement on Adventism[63]—an

---

conquer sin" (G. B. Thomson, "How a Victorious Life Is Attained," *Review and Herald*, 23
Mar. 1922, p. 6).

56. E.g., Meade MacGuire, *Review and Herald*, 11 Nov. 1920, pp. 24-7. MacGuire says: "In
exactly the same manner [as they are freed from the condemnation and penalty of sin] may
they obtain freedom from the power and dominion of sin" (p. 25).

57. Pease, *By Faith Alone*, p. 183. Pease says that the emphasis was "wholesome."

58. See ibid., p. 189, where Pease speaks of Daniells as "one of the most influential,
respected men in the church."

59. Daniells, *Christ Our Righteousness*, p. 15.

60. Ibid., p. 66, esp. Daniells' comment on Rom. 5:1.

61. Ibid., pp. 66, 108-9. Cf. p. 91.

62. Ibid., pp. 72-3. The statement by Pease, "It is hard to imagine how the doctrine of
justification by faith could have been given greater emphasis" (Pease, *By Faith Alone*,
p. 189), can only be marveled at.

63. "... to receive the Lord Jesus ... not merely as forgiveness of my sins ... but to receive
Him as my Lord, my Righteousness and my very life. ... The Christian life ... is the actual
life of Jesus Christ Himself in my flesh" (Carlyle B. Haynes, *Righteousness in Christ*,
pp. 5-10, 16, 17). "When the life has been cleansed from sin, and *Jesus Christ is in full
control*, the glorious fruits of righteousness will appear..." (W. H. Branson, *The Way to
Christ*, p. 59). "The experience of justification and of sanctification means receiving Jesus
Christ the justifier and the sanctifier, who is Himself our justification and our sanctification [i.e., inwardly]" (W.W. Prescott, *The Saviour of the World*, p. 37). "... when faith
receives Him, Christ's character is appropriated by the believer. *This word is the message
of the Gospel* ..." (M. C. Wilcox, *Studies in Romans*, p. 39). "By accepting Christ we are
reconciled to God. We are justified (made righteous) by His blood from the sins of the past;
we are saved by His indwelling life from continuing in sin" (idem, *The More Abundant Life*,
pp. 47-8). "... [justification] includes forgiveness, ... regeneration, ... and ... it imputes

influence whose major emphasis was on the indwelling Christ who will live *His* life in and through the believer.

To vindicate the character of God from the charges of Satan by proving that the law of God can be adequately kept, even by feeble mortals suffering the effects of six thousand years of sin, became the ultimate challenge of Adventist perfectionism. This perfectionism attained its clearest expression in the teaching of the theologian, M.L. Andreasen:[64]

> It is in the last generation of men living on the earth that God's power unto sanctification will stand fully revealed. The demonstration of that power is God's vindication. It clears Him of any and all charges which Satan has placed against Him. In the last generation God is vindicated and Satan defeated.[65]

> In the last generation God will stand vindicated. In the remnant Satan will meet his defeat. The charge that the law cannot be kept will be met and fully refuted. God will produce not only one or two who keep His commandments, but a whole group, spoken of as the 144,000. They will have disproved Satan's accusation against the government of heaven.[66]

> Through the last generation of saints God stands finally vindicated. Through them He defeats Satan and wins His case. They form a vital part of the plan of God.[67]

> He [Paul] does not claim absolute perfection, which is equivalent to holiness, but he does claim relative perfection. . . .
> Will any ever attain to the perfection to which Paul said he had not attained? . . .
> But will any ever reach that stage? We believe so. Read the description of the 144,000 in Revelation 14:4, 5. . . .[68]

> Before the end comes God will have a people behind in no good thing. They will reflect the image of God fully.[69]

---

the righteousness of Christ" (I. H. Evans, *This Is the Way*, p. 65). ". . . Christ saves, and by His imparted obedience brings the saved one out from under the curse" (Spalding, *Origin and History*, 2:286).

64. Special attention is drawn to M. L. Andreasen's perfectionism for two reasons: (1) It marks the clearest expression of the main thrust of Adventist teaching in this area prior to 1950. (2) It was clearly repudiated by Seventh-day Adventist leadership in the 1960's but was resurrected in the 1970's.

65. M. L. Andreasen, *The Sanctuary Service*, pp. 303-4.

66. Ibid., p. 315.

67. Ibid., p. 319.

68. M. L. Andreasen, *The Book of Hebrews*, p. 467.

69. Ibid., p. 468.

Summary

Seventh-day Adventists claim to be the special "remnant-heirs" of the Reformers. Notwithstanding this, in the period of 1844-1950 the fundamental theology of the Adventist gospel sometimes has more affinity with the Roman Catholic Council of Trent than with the Protestant Reformers.

Up to this point in our investigation, the crucial area of Adventism's handling of the gospel has been *the relation of justification and sanctification*. The peculiar Adventist understanding of righteousness by faith has influenced the movement's approach to that relation.

Adventist theology from 1844 to 1950 has been confused over the relation of justification and sanctification. The fundamental characteristic of this confusion is the subordination of justification to sanctification. This has sometimes found expression in the definition of justification as including sanctificational renewal. The subordination also has a chronological aspect in that it views justification by imputation of the extrinsic (outside) righteousness of Christ in terms of the *past* only. Justification has had the status of *mere,* while sanctification by inner renewal has been seen as the way of acceptance in the judgment. Hand in hand with this subordination has gone the un-Reformational notion of here-and-now perfectionism. Hence, righteousness by faith has meant *both* justification and sanctification, but mainly sanctification. If there is any difference between the two periods examined thus far, it is that there has been a progression from overt Pelagianism in the earlier period (1844-1888) to a more refined semi-Pelagianism in the latter period (1888-1950).

The semi-Pelagianism of this largely Tridentine approach has perpetrated a serious infringement of *the freedom of God* in Adventist theology. There can be little doubt that this has been mainly caused by the failure of the movement to give the theological priority to Christ, as did the Reformers. The Christological determination of *grace alone* would have gone a long way in maintaining the sovereign divine assumption and the believer's sinfulness. In viewing the evidence, there is not a shadow of doubt that the incarnation is minimized in the Adventist theology of the 1844-1950 period. It is either largely forgotten (1844-1888) or transferred to a new place (1888-1950) — namely, the believer.

Adventism's theology of the gospel between 1844 and 1950 has failed to echo the Reformation understanding of the grace of God as *God Himself in Christ*. The subordination of justification to sanctification has infringed upon the Reformers' distinctive understanding of grace in the following ways:

1. Whereas the Reformers focused their supreme attention on the grace of God in the incarnation, Adventist theology has mainly been hagiocentric (focused on the believer). The Reformation *faith alone* has the "Christ *for* me" as its focus and not the "Christ *in* me." Thus, there is always a looking *away from* the believer rather than *toward* the believer or Christ in the believer, as in Tridentinism and Adventism.

2. The relation of the *alien* grace of God in Christ to the believer was treated by the Reformers in the Chalcedonian framework. But in Adventism (and pietistic evangelicalism, from which Adventism has borrowed its "victorious-life" piety), the relation between Christ (the grace of God) and the believer is suspiciously ambiguous. This is particularly the case after 1888. What is actually meant by "Christ obeying the law in us" or "this [obedience] is not *ours* but Christ's" or "it is all of Him" is, to our knowledge, never spelled out either in Adventism or evangelicalism. It must mean either the total negation of the humanhood of the believer in the interest of deference to Christ, or some type of fusion of Christ and the believer that destroys the properties of each. One thing is clear: the Reformation position of *by faith alone* is not compatible with such a union. It is probable that this "Christ in me" emphasis provides the impetus for the doctrine of perfectionism. After all, if we are not to have a sinful indwelling Christ, we must have a sinless receptacle (the believer). Because the believer is inescapably bound up with the sanctification process, the right relating of justification and sanctification always involves the right relating of Christ and the believer.

Hence, in Adventism's theology of the gospel, righteousness by faith is not only justification *and* sanctification, but *mainly* sanctification. That which in Reformation theology is exclusively justification is made almost exclusively sanctification, with an emphasis upon *prima gratia* which destroys the personhood of the believer.

3. When priority is given to sanctification, as in Adventist theology, the Reformation *simul justus et peccator* (at the same time righteous and a sinner) is eradicated. But when sanctification is kept under the machine-gun fire of justification (Thielicke), the infinite qualitative difference between the grace of God in Christ and the believer is kept in view. On the other hand, if justification is reduced to the role of servant to sanctification, then it is always easier to bridge the gulf that is otherwise fixed between the perfect doing and dying of Christ and the believer's experience. Thus, the *faith alone* of the Reformation was the radicalization of the "otherness" of grace. Of course, one might object that it is the obedience of Christ *in* the believer that stands in the judgment and not the believer himself. But this ontological appropriation of the merits of Christ is at the expense of the believer's humanhood.

It is because of the perspective of *simul justus et peccator* that Luther saw the vindication (or justification) of the believer at the last judgment as the *consummation* of that which has already been inaugurated in Christ.[70] The basis of acceptance at the last is the same as at the beginning of the sanctification process. That which holds the two together is *faith*. It is the extrinsic righteousness of Christ which is the basis of acceptance, and not the righteousness of inner renewal.[71]

This approach provides a striking contrast with Adventism. Generally speaking, prior to 1888 the beginning of the sanctification process was forgiveness of past sins through the *death* of Christ, while the ability to stand in the last judgment was based on the law-keeping *obedience* of the believer. After 1888 this was refined. The doing and dying of Christ was the basis of acceptance at beginning and end, but it was the doing and dying of Christ *in* the believer and not the doing and dying of Christ *for* the believer. Luther's *sola fide* (faith alone) was obscured.

It remains to be seen how the "last-day heirs of the Reformers" fare in the modern period of the movement.

---

70. See T. F. Torrance and J. K. S. Reid, eds., "Eschatology," *"Scottish Journal of Theology" Occasional Papers*, no. 2, p. 41.
71. See Luther, *Luther's Works*, 25:262; 26:9, 231-32, 235-36.

Part III

Adventism
and the
Reformation
after 1950

Introduction to Part III

We have depicted the history of Seventh-day Adventism as the history of a struggle to be faithful to its goal of furthering the work of an arrested Reformation. In the contemporary era this ongoing struggle does not lessen but intensifies. Significant features emerge, including a polarization within the church concerning what constitutes the heart of true Adventism.

Some preliminary information about the period as a whole will help to keep its important aspects in proper perspective:

1. As we might expect from the material examined thus far, a burning issue of the contemporary period is the message of 1888. In some respects it is a period of *return* to 1888, though this return is by no means uniform in nature.

2. The modern period of Adventism is one in which the contrast between the theology of the Reformers and that of the Roman Catholic Council of Trent is shown as never before in the movement's history. These two theological approaches to the gospel

constitute the polarization referred to above.

3. It will be helpful to approach contemporary Adventism according to the decades it embraces. Each decade (for practical purposes we are classifying the 1970's as a decade) has its own distinctive contribution to make. For this reason we shall here give a brief overview of the entire period.

The modern era in Adventism is definitely different in important aspects from all that has gone before. Hence, it is *new* in a very real sense. In fact, it would not be wide of the mark to say that the present period of the 1970's is the *kairos*-time (the time of opportunity) for Seventh-day Adventism as far as its goal is concerned.

The 1950's was the decade of *Christological advancement* and a return to the *catholic*[1] element of 1888. This advancement was spearheaded by LeRoy Edwin Froom and Roy Allan Anderson, but not without opposition. The opposition came largely from M.L. Andreasen in his *Letters to the Churches*, published toward the end of the decade.

The decade of the 1960's was a time of *soteriological advancement*, which was dependent upon the advancement of the previous decade. The 1960's witnessed an attempt to return to the soteriological message of 1888. There was intense dialogue between, on the one hand, what is known in Adventism as the "Awakening" and, on the other hand, the church administration and Adventist theologians. In certain important respects this decade broke with major emphases in Adventist thought prior to the modern era.

The period of the 1970's is one of *polarization and crisis*, brought about by a breakthrough into Reformation theology on the one hand, and by a return to pre-1950 Adventism on the other. The Christological and soteriological advancements of the previous two decades have received quite different treatments in the 1970's. Those who take the Reformation stream of thought see themselves as taking the findings of the previous two decades to their necessary conclusion. Those who have returned to pre-1950 Adventism have had to repudiate the progress of the 1950's and the 1960's. The 1970's is therefore the period of crisis for the Seventh-day Adventist Church — a crisis which concerns the nature of true Adventism.

---

1. In this sense, *catholic* does not mean *Roman Catholic* but *the universal Christian church*.

5

Off to an Auspicious Start: The 1950's[1]

Around the very beginning of the contemporary period, the feeling was again present among some influential Adventist leaders that all was not well with the "remnant" movement that had been called by God to further the arrested Reformation of the sixteenth century. The "loud cry" had not been given. The Lord had not come. In this respect the time to which we refer was akin to the period prior to 1888 when Ellen G. White was drawing attention to the Laodicean state of the movement.

Ernest D. Dick gives an interesting diagnosis of the problem in the publication, *Aflame for God*.[2] He writes on the topic, "The Heart of Our Message."[3] Dick says, "Righteousness by faith [is] the heart of the [Adventist] message," and he points out that this was the basic issue in the Protestant Reformation and in the 1888

---

1. This title, "Off to an Auspicious Start," is taken from *Aflame for God*, addresses and panel discussion of the 1950 pre-session council of the Seventh-day Adventist Ministerial Association. In 1950, at San Francisco, Calif., thousands of Adventist leaders and ministers from all over the world gathered together for the quadrennial General Conference Session of the church. The Ministerial Association conducted a pre-session which addressed itself to the theme, "Christ-Centered Preaching."

2. See n. 1 above.

3. *Aflame for God*, pp. 81-8.

Minneapolis General Conference Session.[4] However, from 1844-1888, says Dick, the Adventist Church had not experienced Christ-centered preaching and had therefore fallen prey to legalism and a low spiritual tone.[5] Dick cites Mrs. White, who said that "the doctrine of justification by faith has been lost sight of by many who have professed to believe in the third angel's message."[6] But what of the time up to 1950? Dick says, "We have *not yet* laid hold of that important message of the 1888 conference as God would have us. ..."[7] The church was still in the Laodicean state.

Roy A. Anderson urged that the answer to the dilemma lay in "Christ-centered preaching," and he adduced much support from the writings of Mrs. White to show that Jesus should be the center of every doctrine—a fact which, as Dick pointed out, much traditional Adventist preaching and teaching had not honored to the degree it should have. Ministers of the gospel must be "aflame for God." This emphasis was given expression in Seventh-day Adventist study conferences both in the United States and Australia. It was believed that this Christ-centered preaching was what the church lacked. It would revive her out of the "poor and naked state" in which she largely stood.

Robert J. Wieland returned from his post in Africa and encountered the Christ-centered preaching emphasis with its attendant fervor and enthusiasm. But he was not impressed. As far as he was concerned, the church was in confusion—a confusion which expressed itself in the failure to distinguish the difference between preaching Christ and preaching antichrist. To Wieland, this "new" emphasis was no better than the way of the "Babylonians" (i.e., evangelical Protestant denominations).[8] This was expressed by Mr. Wieland in a letter to the General Conference of the church. Naturally, the leaders were shocked at the suggestion.

Wieland followed up his letter with a monograph prepared in

---

4. Ibid., p. 82.

5. Ibid., p. 85.

6. Ibid.

7. Ibid., p. 86. Emphasis supplied.

8. This comment by Wieland (and his subsequent writings) reflects a feeling—shared by not a few Adventists—of suspicion toward modern evangelical Protestantism. Granted that much modern Protestantism is deserving of criticism, Mr. Wieland nevertheless tends to regard *all* Protestantism as suspect.

company with D. K. Short. *1888 Re-examined* was presented to the officers of the General Conference as a private manuscript. The fact is, however, that it infiltrated the wider constituency of Adventists and caused no little stir. The material was explosive. The authors had gained access to facts concerning 1888 which had not reached the ears of Adventists prior to this time. As indicated in Appendix A of *A Warning and Its Reception*, this manuscript brought forth formal replies from the General Conference of the church. Here, in *1888 Re-examined*, was the assertion that the trouble with the church was her rejection of the message of the Lord in 1888. She was called to corporate confession of her guilt.

While the "Christ-centered preaching" motif could have become little more than a cliché to many, it appears that L. E. Froom and R. A. Anderson felt constrained to give the matter some substance. Dr. Froom, being a historian, became convinced that the Adventist movement prior to 1888 had lacked true catholicity. He viewed 1888 as an attempt to get the church established on what he called the "eternal verities" (the Trinity, the deity of Christ, the humanity of Christ, and the atonement). Froom saw 1888 as an advance in that it purged the movement of anti-Trinitarianism and Arianism. But he also saw that the opposition of Adventist conservatism had prevented a restoration of *all* the "eternal verities." Froom thought it was time for Adventism to move forward again by an uninhibited confession of Christ's sinless human nature and finished atonement.

It is important to note that Froom's emphasis concerning 1888 was *catholicity* and not justification by faith. Thus, the first event of great significance in the contemporary period was a focusing on catholicity.

At this time of renewed ferment over the whole question of 1888, two evangelical scholars made their way to the Adventist leaders to clarify their thinking on the actual status of Adventism. (Was it a cult or an evangelical church?) Donald Grey Barnhouse and Walter Martin were warmly received at General Conference headquarters.

The major concerns of Barnhouse and Martin were (1) the human nature of Christ, (2) the atonement, (3) the concept of "Babylon," and (4) the idea of the "remnant." After discussion, Barnhouse and Martin were surprised and somewhat impressed at the answers they received on these aspects of theology. Froom and Anderson denied that Adventism had fundamentally taught either the sinful nature of Christ or that the atonement had not been completed at the cross. Froom said that such deviations belonged to what he called the "lunatic fringe" of the church.[9] One only had to note the many statements from Mrs. White concerning the sinless nature of Christ and His atonement on the cross. Thus, Barnhouse and Martin were satisfied that the Seventh-day Adventist movement should be recognized as an evangelical denomination in spite of its heterodox features (e.g., the non-immortality of the soul).

This was a historic meeting for Adventism. There had not been a meeting like it since the inception of the movement. The leaders of the church (in actual fact, the authors were apparently L. E. Froom, R. A. Anderson, and W. E. Read) published the historic volume, *Seventh-day Adventists Answer Questions on Doctrine.*[10] Walter Martin published a book called *The Truth About Seventh-day Adventism*.

This historic meeting and the publication of *Questions on Doctrine* brought a mixed reception among Adventists. Some welcomed the turn of events as at last vindicating the movement as a legitimate evangelical denomination, while others (e.g., M. L. Andreasen) saw it as "selling the movement down the river."[11] A. L. Hudson in *Witnessing a Metamorphosis*[12] saw the Adventist

---

9. The historical facts will not support Froom's alibi. Prior to the 1950's almost all Adventist authors taught the sinful nature of Christ and His uncompleted work of atonement.

10. Hereafter *Questions on Doctrine*.

11. E.g., M. L. Andreasen in his *Letters to the Churches* opposed *Questions on Doctrine* on the incarnation and the atonement. Cf. Roy Allan Anderson, "Human, Not Carnal," *The Ministry*, Sept. 1956, pp. 14-15. Cf. also Francis D. Nichol, *Answers to Objections*, for the doctrine of the atonement from 1888 to the 1950's.

12. This work is a compilation of articles by Donald Grey Barnhouse and Walter Martin appearing in *Eternity* magazine and articles by E. Schuyler English and Walter Martin appearing in *Our Hope* magazine. There is also the record of a conversation between Barnhouse and A. L. Hudson "relative to the relationship between the editors of *Eternity* magazine and the General Conference of Seventh-day Adventists" (pt. 3). It is claimed that Barnhouse and Martin gave assurance to Hudson that they had received written approval of the accuracy of their articles *before* they were published. The significance of this citation lies in the fact that there is considerable disagreement among Adventists concerning just how official *Questions on Doctrine* actually is. Some take the position that it is as official as any publication that has been put out by the General Conference of the church, while others take the view that it merely represents the opinions of a few very catholic-minded church leaders. This difference of opinion remains even to the present and

church undergoing a metamorphosis from a cult status to a recognized evangelical status, and he was obviously unhappy with the new fraternity.

An examination of *Christianity Today* around the time will show that Adventists were not the only ones who were divided over the status of Adventism and the significance of the Barnhouse and Martin meeting with the General Conference leaders.[13]

Questions on Doctrine was a notable turn in the direction of the Reformation on what Froom called the "eternal verities."[14] Definite advancement took place on the subjects of the *incarnation* and the *atonement*. In this respect the book furthered an important aspect of the revival of 1888.[15] This fact gives to the contemporary

is significant in no small degree for the latest phase of the crisis within Adventism concerning the nature and meaning of righteousness by faith. We shall have occasion at a later stage to point out the precise relation of *Questions on Doctrine* to the present conflict.

13. *Christianity Today* carried quite a full coverage of the *Questions on Doctrine* publication and related subjects, giving both evangelicals and Adventists the opportunity to express their opinions. See John H. Gerstner, "Current Religious Thought," *Christianity Today*, 3 Mar. 1958, p. 39; Harold Lindsell, "What of Seventh-day Adventism?" pt. 1, ibid., 31 Mar. 1958, pp. 6-8 (At this time Lindsell was dean of the faculty at Fuller Theological Seminary, Pasadena, Calif.); O. J. Ritz, "The Problem of Prejudice," ibid., 31 Mar. 1958, pp. 8f.; Lindsell, "What of Seventh-day Adventism," pt. 2, ibid., 14 Apr. 1958, pp. 13f.; Herbert S. Bird, "Another Look at Adventism," ibid., 28 Apr. 1958, p. 14; "Adventists and Others," in "Eutychus and His Kin," ibid., 12 May 1958, p. 23; "Adventist Avalanche," in "Eutychus and His Kin," ibid., 26 May 1958, p. 16; Frank H. Yost, "A Seventh-day Adventist Speaks Back," ibid., 21 July 1958, pp. 15-18; "First Day of the Week," in "Eutychus and His Kin," ibid., 21 July 1958, pp. 25-6; Herbert S. Bird, "Reply to an Adventist," ibid., 18 Aug. 1958, pp. 24-5; Frank A. Lawrence, "Exhaustive Research," book review of Walter Martin, *The Truth About Seventh-day Adventism*, ibid., 4 July 1960, p. 36; Walter Martin, "*Questions on Doctrine*: A Cleft in Seventh-day Adventism?" editorial, ibid., 19 Dec. 1960, p. 24; Francis D. Nichol, "On the Fringe" (written by Nichol, editor of the *Review and Herald*, concerning Martin's book), and Walter Martin, reply to Nichol, ibid., 30 Jan. 1961, p. 16; Francis D. Nichol, "Reminder to Rejoinder," ibid., 13 Mar. 1961, pp. 19-20; "Adventist Literature," ibid., 26 Mar. 1961, p. 38; Walter Martin, "Years Too Late," book review of Herbert S. Bird, *Theology of Seventh-day Adventism*, ibid., 2 Mar. 1962 (Martin's point is that Bird did not research contemporary Adventist literature, otherwise he would have realized that Adventists had expunged the Christological aberrations that Bird charged them with.); Harold Lindsell, "The Best Four-in-One," book review of Hoekema, *Four Major Cults*, ibid., 31 Jan. 1964 (Lindsell criticizes an otherwise excellent book because it takes no note of the "Brinsmead brothers" and the Awakening agitation, which will be treated later in this book.); A. J. Escobar (an Adventist), "Eschatology — Great Divider," ibid., 27 Mar. 1964, p. 21.

14. See esp. "Questions About Christ" and "Questions on Christ and His Ministry in the Sanctuary," *Questions on Doctrine*, pp. 33-86, 339-445. See also appendixes, pp. 641-92, for Ellen G. White citations on controverted issues between evangelicals and Adventists.

15. The human nature of Christ and the nature of the atonement were the matters left unsettled in 1888.

era a distinct superiority over the previous two periods we have looked at.

The importance of *Questions on Doctrine* is less, however, when we come to ask whether or not there is advancement over the previous two periods on the Adventist articulation of justification by faith. There is no significant advance in the volume on *soteriology* (the doctrine of salvation) and, in particular, on *grace*.[16] The book subordinates justification to sanctification and embraces what Niebuhr called "the Augustinian view of grace":

> ... That one is justified, not by obedience to the law, but by the grace that is in Christ Jesus. By accepting Christ, man is reconciled to God, justified by His blood *for the sins of the past*, and saved from the power of sin *by His indwelling life*.[17]

The section just quoted is followed by the statement:

> Thus the gospel becomes "the power of God unto salvation. ..." This experience is wrought by the divine agency of the Holy Spirit. ... The honor and merit of *this wonderful transformation* belong wholly to Christ.[18]

Since Dr. Froom was one of the authors of *Questions on Doctrine*, it is not surprising to find him speaking of "initial justification" in his later *Movement of Destiny*.[19]

It was undoubtedly the firm conviction of Dr. Froom that the whole matter of the Adventists' relation to the "eternal verities" had to be put right. With his usual thoroughness he documented the great lack in this area in the pre-1888 period of the move-

---

16. The difference between *Questions on Doctrine* and the Reformation on *grace* may be seen in the following quotation from under the heading, "Bible Definition ... of Grace": "This is the grace of God in its peculiar New Testament sense. It is God's unlimited, all-inclusive, transforming love toward sinful men and women; and the good news of this grace, as revealed in Jesus Christ, is 'the power of God unto salvation' (Rom. 1:16). *It is not merely God's mercy and willingness to forgive, but it is an active, energizing, transforming power to save.* Thus it may fill a person (John 1:14), it may be given (Rom. 12:3, 6), it is all-sufficient (2 Cor. 12:9; compare Rom. 5:20), it reigns (Rom. 5:21), it teaches (Titus 2:11, 12), it establishes the heart (Heb. 13:9). In some instances 'grace' seems almost to be equivalent to 'gospel' (Col. 1:6) and to the working of God generally (Acts 11:23; 1 Peter 5:12)" (*Questions on Doctrine*, pp. 137-38). Emphasis supplied.

17. "Fundamental Beliefs of Seventh-day Adventists," *Questions on Doctrine*, p. 13. Emphases supplied.

18. Ibid. Emphases supplied.

19. Froom, *Movement of Destiny*, p. 650.

ment,[20] obviously believing that the rectification in *Questions on Doctrine* would finally honor the 1888 message in Adventism. Hence, in LeRoy Edwin Froom we have a going back to the *catholic* emphasis of 1888. Yet while this going back must not be under-estimated as to its significance for the Adventist movement, it seems that Dr. Froom did not realize that it is possible to be a "catholic" and still be a "Roman Catholic" in one's soteriology.

Questions on Doctrine clarified the position of Adventists as Christians in the eyes of many who up to this point were somewhat doubtful. But in terms of any real advance on the theology of the Reformation gospel, its significance was limited. Whereas the "catholicizing" of the movement made it clear that Adventists were Christians, it did not make it clear that they were Christians standing in the worthy line of the Reformation rather than in the Roman Catholic tradition. *Questions on Doctrine* did little to sub-stantiate the Adventist claim to be special heirs of the Reformers. However, Dr. Froom apparently did not realize this.

The soteriological inadequacy of *Questions on Doctrine* concern-ing righteousness by faith is reflected elsewhere in the period. For all the good intentions of *Aflame for God*, it does nothing to en-hance Adventism as being a great exponent of justification by faith. It contains much talk about the need to preach the message, but seldom does one find a passage which even clearly seeks to outline what that message is. Ernest Dick's contribution on "The Heart of Our Message,"[21] mentioned at the beginning of this chap-ter, is a case in point. Dick says that the message of the Adventist movement is "...justification by faith; ... sanctification by faith; ... glorification by faith; ... all of it together... is righteousness by faith"![22]

The view of justification as only for the sins of the past was clearly indicated, for example, by the Executive Committee of the Australasian Division of Seventh-day Adventists in 1959. We read:

> The *experience* of justification is often spoken of as imputed right-eousness. Justification or imputed righteousness deals *only with*

---

20. See ibid., pp. 148-87. Yet see pp. 526, 530 for Froom's endorsement of E. J. Waggoner's *Glad Tidings* and his other books.
21. *Aflame for God*, pp. 81-8.
22. Ibid., p. 84.

the past. Sanctification or imparted righteousness deals *only with the present and future*. Justification is God's method of dealing with *a man's past life of sin*.[23]

Likewise, A.V. Olson in *Through Crisis to Victory* shows that he does not understand the Pauline or Reformation doctrine when he cites the position of G. I. Butler—a position obviously at odds with the Reformation—to prove that he believed in righteousness by faith.[24] Olson also quotes J. H. Waggoner's comments on Romans 3:21 to show that he really believed in righteousness by faith as well. Here Waggoner says that the righteousness of God means His own attributes, the revelation of His will, "and thirdly, ... the righteousness of his saints, whose characters are made conformable to his will. In this latter sense it is used in 2 Cor. 5:21, 'That we might be made the righteousness of God in him'. ..."[25] These old Adventist statements, cited approvingly by Olson, are inimical to the position of true Protestantism, but they are a fairly good expression of classical Romanism.

In his *Drama of the Ages*, W. H. Branson reveals his belief that acceptance in the final judgment is on the basis of the law-keeping of the believer:

> But since the law does exist, it serves as a witness to the righteousness of those who, through the power of the indwelling Christ, comply with its requirements. ...
>
> That is to say, when a man breaks even one of the least of the commandments and teaches others that it is not necessary for them to keep the moral law, God and the holy angels in heaven count that man least among the people of earth. He is established in sin. But when a man keeps them—all of them—himself and teaches others the importance of this obligation, the heavenly host look upon him with approbation. He is called "great" in the kingdom of heaven. This will be the basis of the decisions in the final judgment.
>
> "This is the end of the matter; all hath been heard: fear God, and keep his commandments; for this is the whole duty of man." Ecclesiastes 12:13, ARV. A Christian who through faith in Jesus

---

23. Executive Committee of the Australasian Division, *Righteousness by Faith*, pp. 7-8. Emphases supplied.
24. Olson, *Through Crisis to Victory*, pp. 45-7.
25. The section Olson cites is from *Review and Herald*, 23 Sept. 1884, pp. 616-17.

Christ has faithfully kept the law's requirements will be acquitted; there is no condemnation, for the law finds no fault in him.[26]

In the significant Bible conference convened by the church in 1952,[27] Dr. Edward Heppenstall presented a paper called "The Covenants and the Law."[28] In this he sees righteousness by faith as being justification *and* sanctification, but mainly the latter:

> The other method of bringing harmony between man and the law is to change the sinful nature of man, so that it becomes again in accord with the divine law. There is only one method by which this can be done. That is the method of free grace, or righteousness by faith.
>
> Therefore, if we depend upon God's power, the method is one of grace.[29]

For Dr. Heppenstall, "the gospel works holiness in man." It is what God does in the soul.[30] Heppenstall sees the contrast between *letter* and *spirit* as a contrast between "righteousness by works" and "righteousness by faith."[31]

Dr. Froom, for all his stature (within and without Adventism), concurs with traditional Adventist teaching when it asserts that acceptance in the judgment is based at least partly upon the inward obedience of the believer (wrought, of course, by Christ):

---

26. Branson, *Drama of the Ages*, p. 308.

27. Reported in *Our Firm Foundation*.

28. Edward Heppenstall, "The Covenants and the Law," in *Our Firm Foundation*, 1:435-92. See pp. 464, 484, 489.

29. Ibid., p. 464. This is the Augustinian view of grace and not the true Protestant view.

30. "The law and the gospel become inseparable as light and heat in the sun. God demands obedience under the law. God works obedience through the gospel. The law of God demands holiness of men. The gospel works holiness in men. As long as the law remains written merely on stone, men find the commandments hard to obey. While the heart is stony, the commandments appear stony" (ibid., p. 484).

31. "In the third place, the fact that the Holy Spirit writes the law of God on the mind and heart proclaims in no unmistakable terms that this experience comes only by supernatural means and never by naturalistic means. The issue between letter and spirit, between righteousness by works and righteousness by faith, is this: Does man save himself, or does God save him? The union of the law and the gospel in the life is something that God does for man, and that man cannot possibly do for himself" (ibid). "The Sabbath commandment, more than any of the others, signifies the unity of the law and the gospel. It signifies the rest of the completed work of God in the soul, the rest of righteousness by faith. It is the seventh-day Sabbath that is appealed to throughout Israel's history as the test of the work of the Spirit through the everlasting covenant" (p. 489).

4. *Christ's Perfect Obedience and Righteousness.* —Meticulous and intensive obedience to the moral law will never produce the requisite Righteousness in us, without which no one can endure in the presence of a holy God. It is only the perfect obedience and spotless Righteousness of Christ —as God and man —both imputed and imparted to us, that will satisfy the demands of the sacred law and the requirements of a holy God.[32]

Notwithstanding that in the 1950's *Questions on Doctrine* turned toward the true catholicism of the Reformers, the Adventist community did not correct the failure in the preceding years of its history to make good its claim to be the *special* heirs of the Reformation gospel. This is further indicated by the presence of *perfectionism* in the era of the 1950's.

Perfectionism is to be found in more than one contributor to *Our Firm Foundation*.[33] W. H. Branson deals with *imputed* and *imparted* righteousness.[34] On the former he appears to be quite Protestant. But when he moves on to discuss the latter, he shows himself to be at variance with Reformation thought. Following the fundamental direction of the movement from 1888 onward, Branson sees the demands of the law as being met by the *Christ within*:

> And what is to be the result of the abiding presence of Christ in the human heart and life? He is to *work* in us, doing the will of God through us. "It is God which worketh in you." Phil. 2:13. By Christ's living and working in us we shall "be filled with all the fulness of God." Eph. 3:19.[35]

In our brief theological appraisal of the previous two periods, we mentioned that the relation between the indwelling Christ and the believer is always (suspiciously) ambiguous. Here is a classic example from Branson:

> He is able to do "exceeding abundantly." We can do nothing, but He is mighty to save. His omnipotence is united with our humanity, and our success in producing righteousness is in accordance with "the power that worketh in us." Since that power is now Christ, our

---

32. Froom, *Movement of Destiny*, p. 670.

33. *Our Firm Foundation* is a report of the Seventh-day Adventist Bible conference held Sept. 1-13, 1952, in the Sligo Seventh-day Adventist Church, Takoma Park, Md.

34. W. H. Branson, "The Lord Our Righteousness," in *Our Firm Foundation*, 2:573-618.

35. Ibid., p. 594.

lives will reflect His virtues and beauty. *He is able.*[36]

Does this mean that we have a peccable Christ or an impeccable believer?[37] Branson is explicit:

> Perfection, then, is possible for us. The God who demonstrated His power by bringing Jesus from the dead can also make you perfect—perfect in every good work to do His will. How is this accomplished? It is by Christ working within us. He does within us and through us the things that are well-pleasing in God's sight.
>
> Thus we receive His righteousness. It still does not come by our own works but by what He does for us and through us.[38]
>
> *A Transformation*
>
> This experience brings *an entire transformation of life*. We become partakers of *the divine nature*, and the virtues of Christ take the place of the works of the flesh.[39]

Further on in the same work, Branson spells out his logic: "So long as Christ remains in full control, sin is not committed, since He is not a sinner."[40]

J. H. Jemison, in the same *Our Firm Foundation*,[41] develops in a most explicit fashion the concept of M. L. Andreasen that the final generation will match the Saviour in sinlessness of character.[42]

Though we shall not go into an exposition of Edward Heppenstall's position in his contribution to *Our Firm Foundation* on "The Covenants and the Law,"[43] it is important to note that it

---

36. Ibid. Emphasis in original.

37. Not to raise the further question of whether or not we have a new hypostatic union here!

38. Branson, "The Lord Our Righteousness," in *Our Firm Foundation*, 2:595.

39. Ibid. Emphases supplied.

40. Ibid., p. 597. Branson, like all perfectionists (i.e., those who believe in here-and-now perfection), does not seem to realize the dilemma that such a position poses. If Christ is in *full* control and the believer sins, then such sin has to be attributed to Christ; otherwise, the *full* control that Christ is said to exercise has to be qualified. This is one of the basic weaknesses of Adventist perfectionism prior to 1950 and of the evangelical "holiness movement" perfectionism, from which Adventism has heavily drawn. This same weakness is evident even in Froom. See LeRoy Edwin Froom, *The Coming of the Comforter,* pp. 144, 150. See also idem, *Movement of Destiny*, pp. 320-22, where Froom acknowledges his debt to the holiness movement.

41. J. H. Jemison, "The Companions of the Lamb," in *Our Firm Foundation*, 2:403-24.

42. "...an experience matching that of the Saviour. ... His life [was] sinless" (ibid., p. 412).

43. See n. 28 above.

seems to be in harmony with the perfectionism of Branson and Jemison. We draw attention to this because Dr. Heppenstall emerges with an anti-perfectionism stance in the next decade.

It is interesting to note still another advocate of perfectionism in the decade of the 1950's—the Defense Literature Committee of the General Conference.[44] (We say "interesting" because the committee later reversed its stance and published *anti*-perfectionism material against the "Awakening" in the 1960's.) The committee approvingly reproduces paragraphs "which appear in a letter received recently from Elder A.W. Spalding, one of our older, experienced and highly honored brethren. ..." One paragraph reads as follows:

> It is clear that this experience [of perfection] has not come to us as a people, and who can claim to see it in himself or in any other individual? This state of perfection, indeed, will not come while we are looking either at ourselves or at other men; it comes only to him whose eyes are fixed upon Christ, who forgets self, who is utterly emptied of self, and who is filled with Christ. "Christ in you the hope of glory."[45]

The Brinsmead Agitation: A Search for the Way to Stand in the Coming Judgment

In many respects the spiritual struggle of Robert D. Brinsmead and his supporters was the microcosm of the Seventh-day Adventist macrocosmic struggle today. An investigation into the "Brinsmead agitation" will therefore provide an important background for what has been said concerning the previous two periods and what is to be said about Adventism's theology of the gospel in the modern era.

We first need to look at some unique features of Adventist eschatology. Like many evangelical pre-millennialists, Adventists believe that the great tribulation will precede the visible second coming of Christ. They call this the "time of trouble"—a time just

---

44. See the Defense Literature Committee's answer to Robert J. Wieland and Donald K. Short, 4 Dec. 1951, in Hudson, *A Warning and Its Reception*, pp. 248-51.
45. Ibid., p. 249. Cf. "... because we have not received the fulness of Christ, therefore we have not finished the work and gone to glory" (p. 250). Cf. also p. 251.

as awesome, perhaps more so, than the coming tribulation expected by other evangelicals. Adventists believe that it begins at the close of human probation, or end of the time of grace, when there will be no Intercessor in the heavenly sanctuary—not even for the saints. Whereas many pre-millennialists believe that God's people will be raptured out of this world before the tribulation, Adventists believe that the saints will have to live through that awful time. Instead of a pre-tribulation rapture, there is to be a special pre-advent judgment of all the professed people of God, and in that "investigative judgment" a "mark" or "seal" of protection will be placed upon the faithful.

Just as other pre-millennialists look for an any-moment secret rapture of the saints out of the world, Adventists look for an any-moment final judgment in heaven to seal the righteous for the time of trouble. They feel that it is their special commission to proclaim everywhere that this "hour of God's judgment is come" (Rev. 14:7). As well as preaching the literal coming of Christ in power and glory, they see it as their great work to prepare people to stand in this judgment and in the coming tribulation, when Christ will no longer be pleading His blood for sinners.

As Norval Pease frankly acknowledges, the Adventist soteriological emphasis falls on sanctification and imparted righteousness rather than on justification and imputed righteousness.[46] Our investigation into Adventist literature of the previous two periods has confirmed that what Pease says is true. As we have noticed, there has been a very strong current of perfectionism running through the movement. It has generally been believed that if one were going to pass through the time of trouble, he would have to be sealed—and only those who would reach a state of moral and spiritual perfection would be sealed.[47] It is true that Adventists have talked about salvation by grace and by Christ's righteousness, but this has generally meant having Christ's *indwelling grace* in order to keep the law well enough to meet the judgment's scrutiny, and having Christ's *indwelling righteousness* (i.e., sanctification). Justification has been seen as only the initial

46. Pease, *By Faith Alone*, p. 207.
47. Official and unofficial Adventist publications advocating this, both past and present, are legion–e.g., Gordon Collier, LeRoy Edwin Froom, W. H. Branson, and M. L. Andreasen.

step taken by the novice Christian. Justification merely makes one a candidate for the "seal," but this supreme attainment depends upon becoming sanctified enough to qualify at God's awful tribunal.

As an example of this emphasis, we only have to recall the teaching of Branson cited near the close of the previous section of this chapter. Branson is rather typical of Adventists who have taught that Christ in them could keep the law just as perfectly as He did two thousand years ago, if only believers would "let Him." The doctrine of original sin has been conspicuous by its absence, especially as simplistic appeal has been made to Christ's power to do "all things."

It was in 1955 that Robert Brinsmead, a young Australian farmer, decided to go to Avondale College to study theology in earnest. He took seriously all the talk of his church about getting ready for the judgment, the time of trouble, and the Lord's coming. For him, the question of "how to stand in the judgment" was a burning issue.[48]

Brinsmead was troubled by the knowledge of original sin in very much the same way as was Dr. Luther in the sixteenth century. In

48. Reminiscing on his college days, Brinsmead said: "I remember an illustration from college to demonstrate the difference between imputed and imparted righteousness. The lecturer would place a glass on the desk in front of the class. Then he would say, 'We are like that, but we need a covering.' Out of his pocket he would take a clean, white handkerchief and cover the glass, remarking that that is justification, the imputed righteousness of Jesus Christ. Then he would say, 'As we remain under the covering of Christ's imputed righteousness, He begins to fill us with His righteousness (imparted righteousness) for sanctification so that we grow more and more like Jesus Christ.'... This dear old man would lift off the handkerchief and take a peek at the glass, explaining, 'As we near the end of time, the close of probation, God takes a look at us.' He would demonstrate by lifting the handkerchief (the imputed righteousness) and looking at the glass. But God would say, 'Ah, no—they are not quite ready yet. They can't stand without imputed righteousness at this juncture; they haven't got enough imparted righteousness, not quite. ... leave it on a little longer.' So God gives His people a little more time. Finally...he would remove the covering, and God would remark, 'There they are. Just like My Son.' Now the strange thing about the illustration was that the glass was just as naked at the end of the demonstration as it was at the beginning. In actual fact he was proving something that he did not mean to prove, and that is that if you take the best saint that ever lived on the earth and remove from him God's covering of...the merits of Jesus Christ, ... *how does he stand?* Like a Laodicean—naked (Rev. 3:17). Now we had some difficulty with this idea, because we were convinced that the hour of God's judgment had come. ... In the most holy place was the holy law of God, which demanded a righteousness...higher than the highest human thought can reach..." (Robert D. Brinsmead, "All Things Are Ready," sermon report, Dec. 1976).

A Review of the Awakening Message he made these revealing comments:

> Back in the 1950's, I came to the settled conviction that this general view of reaching perfection was impossible and futile, whether one looked at certain statements of Inspiration or history, or experience. Because of this doctrine which was still being taught when I went to college in 1955, very few people that I questioned had any real buoyant hope of being able to pass the scrutiny of the soon-coming judgment of the living. It is no exaggeration to say that most lived in real fear and dread of the judgment, having no way of knowing how to be ready except to "try harder by God's grace" and to hope that such judgment would not come too soon.[49]

Brinsmead could not find a great deal of solace in the optimism and simplistic answers of those to whom he looked for counsel. However, he lacked at that time the necessary theological expertise to articulate the problem of original sin. He spoke of the "scars of sin" and the "record of sin," and later, adding a dash of Freudian terminology, he spoke of "subconscious sin."

As already indicated, Brinsmead could find little help within Adventist theology on the subject of original sin. Our investigation into the theology of Adventism has revealed that, apart from some occasional references in Mrs. White,[50] the subject of original sin has been almost entirely absent. Brinsmead therefore turned to the Reformers for guidance.

It seems that Brinsmead was the first within Adventism to develop and set forth the doctrine of original sin in a systematic way.[51] It is clear from his writings that the anthropological problem loomed large in his thinking. This anthropological problem was accentuated, no doubt, by the Adventist teaching on the imminent judgment, the tribulation, and the coming of Christ.

Brinsmead's answer to the problem of original sin became known as the "Awakening message"—an intra-church agitation

---

49. Robert D. Brinsmead, *A Review of the Awakening Message*, pt. 1, p. 4.

50. See Ellen G. White, *Review and Herald*, 16 Apr. 1901; 19 Aug. 1890; 29 Nov. 1887; idem, *Child Guidance*, p. 475; idem, *Testimonies*, 2:710; 3:343; 4:496, 587; idem, *My Life Today*, p. 261; idem, *Great Controversy*, p. 508.

51. See Robert D. Brinsmead, *Sanctuary Institute Syllabus IV: Original Sin*, pp. 5-47. Brinsmead's teaching in this section of the publication is as strong on original sin as one will find anywhere, including Luther and Calvin.

which disturbed Adventism during the decade of the 1960's. When we examine Brinsmead's answer, it turns out to be a curious combination of Reformation Protestantism and an Adventist understanding of the pre-advent judgment. The element of Reformation Protestantism was the doctrine of *justification,* while the Adventist element was the idea that God will *perfect* the final generation of saints before Jesus comes. Brinsmead's works show a monumental effort to harmonize these two streams of thought, to resolve the impossible tension between the Reformation view of *righteousness by faith* and Adventist *perfectionism.*[52] His theology was not a circle with one focal point, but an ellipse with two focal points—Protestant-style justification and a second experience of perfection, Wesley-Adventist style.

The awareness of original sin caused Brinsmead to reject the whole idea of reaching a state of perfection in order to be ready for the judgment. Here was a clear break from the general view of sanctification which we have encountered thus far in our investigation. For Brinsmead, no amount of inward grace or "imparted righteousness" would qualify one to stand in the judgment. *Christ alone* had enough righteousness to pass the final judgment, and, said Brinsmead, He stands in the judgment as the Representative of the believer. Brinsmead put it like this:

> The idea of coming to the judgment in need of mercy or, more especially, that repentant yet sinful men could boldly and gladly enter in by faith in the righteousness of a substitute, was a new thought to many. More than that, it was the most sweet and joyful news that many had ever heard. Neither time nor circumstances, nor the limitations of erroneous conclusions, can efface the memory of souls weeping for sheer joy at the simple revelation that Christ is our righteousness in judgment, that this judgment is *for* us, that the door is open, and that, looking to Christ, we can say, "All things are ready: come unto the marriage."[53]

Brinsmead goes on to intimate, in words reminiscent of Niebuhr, that this discovery was a very *new* way within Adventism, and a way which seemed to deny the power of God to *make* the believer righteous.

---

52. See the syllabus cited in n. 51 above.
53. Brinsmead, *Review of the Awakening Message,* pt. 1, p. 4.

We therefore utterly rejected any here-and-now perfectionism. We clearly perceived that it was impossible within a believer's probationary life, except in Jesus Christ (see *Testimonies,* vol. 4, p. 367). To many it seemed that we were denying the power of the gospel to *make* us perfect now, and in the words of one critic, some derisively spoke of our vain hope of going into judgment "on the coattails of Christ's personal righteousness."[54]

Instead of looking upon the imminent judgment with only fear and dread, Brinsmead taught that it was to be anticipated with great joy and gladness. Believers should say with Luther, "O happy Judgment Day." The following stanzas from the Awakening song book summed up Brinsmead's thought:

> Jesus stands for me in judgment,
>   He the Lamb all bleeding, torn,
> Pleading now for me His merits
>   There before His Father's throne.
>
> Jesus stands for me in judgment,
>   Naught have I to pass the test,
> But in Him is all perfection,
>   He is all my righteousness.[55]

The other element in Brinsmead's theology was *perfectionism.* It will be remembered that the Awakening adherents rejected here-and-now perfection. However, Brinsmead was at this time too steeped in Andreasen's concept of the final generation to deny that those who live in the "time of trouble" would be altogether without sin. In Brinsmead's own words:

Yet at the same time we did not, could not reject the hereditary Adventist idea of being sinless in order to live without Christ's mediation after the close of probation. As far as we were concerned, that part still remained "fundamental Adventism." We concluded that this final "unattainable" experience would be a gift of our Judge's gracious mercy, i.e., effected in God's people by the "final

---

54. Ibid.

55. Robert A. McCurdy, Jr., "Jesus Stands for Me in Judgment," in *Awake and Sing!* p. 4. Cf. Robert D. Brinsmead, *The Open Door,* pp. 4-5; idem, *Tidings of Great Joy,* pp. 15-16. Note the following: "How many are endeavouring to enter the marriage by living up to all the standards of the law! Christ is robbed of His glory. There is only one Man Who can stand in the judgment—the Man Christ Jesus" (idem, *Tidings of Great Joy,* p. 16).

atonement" and latter rain.[56]

As indicated here, the peculiar contribution made by Brinsmead was to see those of the last generation as having original sin blotted out of them in the pre-advent judgment. In other words, what orthodox Protestantism saw as taking place at the second advent of Christ, Brinsmead saw as taking place in the judgment that precedes the advent in Adventist eschatology. Despite what he said about the all-sufficiency of the righteousness of Christ, he still maintained that, after the pre-advent and pre-tribulation judgment, perfectionism would be a reality. Unlike Wesley, who left his "second blessing" hanging in a mystical "nowhere" or "sometime," Brinsmead tied perfection to an imminent eschatological event.

In all of Brinsmead's theology prior to 1970, the two elements of *justification* and *perfection* are both present.[57] They are strange bedfellows indeed! Within the context of the Reformation the former demands the exclusion of the latter, and the latter is inimical to the former because it has no place for the Reformation *simul justus et peccator* (at the same time righteous and a sinner). Before 1970, Brinsmead attempted to hold together "historic Protestantism" and what he saw as "historic Adventism." In his publications some excellent reproduction of Reformation theology is vitiated by an inconsistent eschatological perfectionism.

Notwithstanding the opposition of church leaders to Brinsmead's theology, it appears that he made a lasting contribution within Adventism.[58] There emerged a small group of Adventist scholars who acknowledged the original-sin problem and who said it would remain until the coming of Christ.[59] These scholars op-

------

56. Brinsmead, *Review of the Awakening Message*, pt. 1, p 4.

57. In the early 1960's, Brinsmead did confound justification with regeneration at the point of the sinner's conversion. But his Reformation concept of original sin caused him to articulate a clear teaching of how a believer is accepted in the judgment. He taught that this is solely by the righteousness mediated for him in God's presence. This was the vital and valid aspect of Brinsmead's contribution.

58. Brinsmead's theology was seen as a threat to "denominational integrity." Some attacked Brinsmead because, in their eyes, he was limiting the power of God to ontically sanctify His people.

59. Such scholars were Dr. Edward Heppenstall, Dr. Desmond Ford, and Dr. Hans K. LaRondelle. We have already made reference to LaRondelle's doctoral dissertation on perfectionism under the Reformed scholar, G. C. Berkouwer, at Amsterdam (see chap. 1, n. 16).

posed Brinsmead's *new* approach to perfectionism while he was opposing the *traditional* perfectionism of men like W. H. Branson.

However, despite the contribution of Brinsmead, the agitation became strained and somewhat belligerent. All over the world, people who showed any sympathy with the Awakening message were relieved of their positions and/or removed from church membership.[60]

The situation was somewhat similar to 1888. Those who rejected E. J. Waggoner and A. T. Jones rejected an emphasis that may well have helped future generations make good their claim to be the special heirs of the Reformation gospel. Likewise with Brinsmead. He was striking a high note in Reformation theology—the note of the all-sufficiency of the doing and dying of Christ as man's Representative—a note that Waggoner and Jones had struck. However, Brinsmead had to go outside of the Adventist church, and this fact has made an objective look at his Reformation emphasis the more difficult for those who have remained loyal to their denomination.

Brinsmead Completes the Pilgrimage to Luther and Calvin

In 1970, Brinsmead undertook an intensive investigation of the theology of the Reformers. Not only did he read the Reformers, but he made a study of Roman Catholic theology as well. For the first time he came to understand the real difference between the Reformation and the Roman Catholic Church. He was surprised to learn that Roman Catholics do not teach a bald doctrine of salvation by human merit.

Luther's "Lectures on Galatians" taught Brinsmead the Refor-

---

60. A. L. Hudson was no doubt correct when he said that "the unpleasant controversy was caused by the sinful nature of those advocating the matter and the sinful nature of those resisting the matter." In 1969, Brinsmead wrote: "It would be exceedingly naive and unrealistic to imagine that our discoveries were made known in perfect tact. Unfortunately, the church officials did not look upon our activities with the least degree of benign indulgence. Oppositon was just as swift and enthusiastic as the agitation of the Awakening message" (Robert D. Brinsmead, *The Timing of Revelation 18 and the Perfecting of the Saints: An Answer to Dr. Desmond Ford and Pastor L. C. Naden*, p. 34).

mation meaning of righteousness by faith as being justification *alone*. Previous to this point, he had thought that righteousness by faith meant *imputed* and *imparted* righteousness. Hence, his eschatological perfection was the end (albeit by grace) of a gradual process of sanctification. But now he learned the Reformers' concept of righteousness *by faith*. He saw that righteousness by faith and sinlessness in the believer were mutually exclusive.

Prior to this, none of Brinsmead's critics (not even Heppenstall, Ford, or LaRondelle) had been able to shake his eschatological perfectionism, for they also viewed righteousness by faith as being both justification and sanctification. But now Brinsmead was faced with a serious decision. He had come to see that the Reformation *sola fide* (faith alone) was opposed to *ontic perfectionism* in the historical process, even if it be a last-generation perfectionism. One element or the other had to go. Brinsmead surrendered up his perfectionism and kept the Reformers' *sola fide*.

A study of Brinsmead's theology after this turning point reveals a passionate antagonism toward the medieval *gratia infusa* (infused grace) and all forms of perfectionism. An attempted reconciliation with the leaders of the Adventist Church in 1971 was apparently abortive, and Brinsmead turned his attention to editing *Present Truth* magazine, where he has articulated his discovery of Reformation theology for the past six years. It is the *Present Truth* Brinsmead that now engages the Adventist Church in theological dialogue—a dialogue concerning that which is truest to the movement's purpose in the world.

The theology of Seventh-day Adventism in the 1960's and 1970's—especially (though not exclusively) in the *Review and Herald*—has been theology in dialogue with Brinsmead *without* the church and with those of his supporters *within* the church. It is to this dialogue that we must now turn.

6

Pain and Progress:
The 1960's

The 1960's was a time of conflict in Seventh-day Adventism. Whatever is said, either negatively or positively, must be said against this backdrop. The Adventist Church was in conflict with the Brinsmead "Awakening message," and it was in this dialogue that the major theological features of the decade emerged:

1. As mentioned in chapter five, Brinsmead postponed the work of perfection until the judgment. In response to this, the Adventist leadership advocated a view of sanctification radically more simplistic than that of the sixteenth-century Reformers. Its chief aspect was the absence of any appreciation of the doctrine of original sin. That there might be a real vitiating sinfulness in the believer was simply dismissed. This was *stage one* of the dialogue with the Awakening—a stage when the leaders of the Adventist movement saw the Brinsmead teaching as being *antinomian.*

2. There then emerged what can only be described as the fruit of religious agitation. Some of the church's more outstanding theologians began to express grave misgivings about the whole question of perfection. The first to openly advocate *no perfection in the believer until the second advent of Christ* was Dr. Edward Heppenstall. He saw perfection of the believer as inimical to salvation

by grace alone. Heppenstall's approach—no perfection until the second coming—was one that not only went against the perfectionism of the Brinsmead message, but it was contrary to the traditional Adventist teaching on perfection. It is surprising, therefore, that Heppenstall's teaching went unchallenged (at least publicly) by the leaders of the church. It may be that the conflict with Brinsmead was so fierce that Dr. Heppenstall's radical deviation from traditional Adventism was able to pass unchallenged. Dr. Desmond Ford and Pastor L. C. Naden were among others who adopted the new approach to perfection against the Brinsmead teaching. This was *stage two* in the conflict with the Awakening— a stage marked by positive gains if measured by the gospel of the Reformation. In this phase of the conflict there was a serious recognition of original sin and no uncertain repudiation of perfectionism. These two aspects of the 1960's constitute a *soteriological advance* of Seventh-day Adventism toward the fulfillment of its avowed goal—namely, to further the arrested Reformation of the sixteenth century.

3. There was evidence in the 1960's of a real effort to "make good" the Adventist aim of giving the gospel to a dying world and an apostate Protestantism. It is difficult to say how much the conflict with the Awakening influenced this deliberate attempt to present the gospel, void of legalism and un-Protestant elements. Very possibly it was sincerely believed that the best antidote to Brinsmeadism was the forthright presentation of the gospel, especially since the conflict must have appeared to many as little more than theologians squabbling over irrelevant theoretical abstractions. But whatever the reasons, the decade was *encouraging* in view of some of the teaching on the gospel to be found among Adventists.

4. Notwithstanding the previous three points, the 1960's was also a time of *confusion*. While struggling to be Protestant, the church also evidenced other irreconcilable streams in her teaching. For example, in the *Review and Herald* articles of the period there coexisted—presumably in a happy fashion—an obvious attempt to follow the Protestant heritage of salvation by grace, together with clear expressions of Tridentine theology. What is more, in the church's defense of her teaching against the

Brinsmead Awakening, the one fountain issued forth material which was mutually exclusive. There are three possibilities open to the interpreter of this phenomenon: (1) It may be that the conflicting nature of the material was not perceived. (2) Perhaps the conflicting nature of the material was perceived, but it was thought that this was a fair price to pay for the removal of the Awakening threat. (3) It may be that the conflicting material was a tacit admission of church leaders that there legitimately existed within the "remnant" church quite different views concerning the core of her confession. Whatever happens to be the correct interpretation is secondary to our aim of observing this contradictory feature of Adventist theology in the last decade.

Before we proceed with a closer examination of this period, we need to relate some of its features to those of the previous decade. The *soteriological* gains of the 1960's (a recognition of original sin and renunciation of perfectionism in this life) build on and carry forward the *Christological* gains of *Questions on Doctrine*. But the 1960's is also an advance over *Questions on Doctrine*, which had a decidedly perfectionistic flavor. In the 1960's, perfectionism is repudiated and the Christology of *Questions on Doctrine* is followed through to some important soteriological implications.

The Negative Aspect of the 1960's

As we have pointed out, the Seventh-day Adventist Church was in conflict with the Brinsmead teaching in the 1960's,[1] and that conflict may be divided into two stages. In the early part of the decade Brinsmead was opposed because he postponed the experience of

---

1. A sample of the material put out in the conflict with the Brinsmead teaching is as follows: Robert D. Brinsmead, *A Doctrinal Analysis of "The History and Teaching of Robert Brinsmead";* idem, *Timing of Revelation 18;* Francis F. Bush, *How a Pastor Meets the Brinsmead Issue; Errors of the Brinsmead Teachings;* Paul H. Freeman, ed., *Evaluation of Brinsmead Doctrine;* Edward Heppenstall, "Some Theological Considerations of Perfection"; A. M. Karolyi, *Errors of the Brinsmead Teachings;* L. C. Naden, *What Do the Brinsmead Faction Really Believe?;* Lauri Onjukka, *The Sanctuary and Perfection;* E. N. Sargeant, *Brinsmead;* John A. Slade, *Lessons from a Detour: A Survey of My Experience in the Brinsmead Movement;* Defense Literature Committee of the General Confererence, *Perfection;* idem, *Some Current Errors in Brinsmead Teachings;* idem, *The History and Teaching of Robert Brinsmead.*

reaching moral perfection until the judgment. But in the latter stage of the conflict Brinsmead was opposed because he wished to maintain, beside his adherence to the Reformation, what he believed was traditional, historic Adventism on the question of final-generation perfection. We are taking up the early stage of the conflict under the heading, "The *Negative* Aspect of the 1960's."[2]

Brinsmead contended that sinful depravity remains in the regenerate until the judgment. But this contention was rejected on the grounds that it denied the power of the gospel and the cleansing power of the Holy Spirit to eradicate sin from the believer *now*. Brinsmead was regarded as *antinomian* and, therefore, a dangerous influence on the members of the remnant community. In the words of Pastor L.C. Naden, the Brinsmead faction

> ... overlook the transforming power of the gospel ministered by the Holy Spirit that makes us new creatures in Him and prepares us for the judgment. Their teaching denies that it is possible for a man to gain complete victory over sin before he appears in the judgment. ... Thank God that the perfecting process is completed before we get into the judgment; if it were not then we would be in a hopeless and helpless position.[3]

The Defense Literature Committee of the General Conference accused the Awakening of denying the *present* power and provision of the gospel:

> We warn our dear people not to be lulled to sleep by the dangerous doctrine that we can expect to come up before the scrutiny of the Judge of all the earth in the investigative judgment, be found wanting, and then expect Christ to cleanse the soul temple by a miracle in order that we may be accounted worthy of eternal life.[4]

Brinsmead complained of being seriously misrepresented.[5] He contended that the issue was not whether one needs to be *converted* or not before the judgment, but whether or not one continues to be a

---

2. "Negative" is not meant to imply a value judgment. It is a statement of the nature of the output when measured against the Reformation gospel, which Adventists claim to have inherited more than any other Christians.

3. Naden, *Brinsmead Faction,* pp. 1, 4. See also Brinsmead, *Timing of Revelation 18,* pp. 34-6.

4. Defense Literature Committee, *History and Teaching,* p. 37.

5. Brinsmead, *Doctrinal Analysis,* p. 32.

sinner until the judgment. Yet the Defense Literature Committee, even as late in the decade as 1967, regarded the Awakening teaching as putting off *"the work which must be done today."*[6]

It appears that the teaching of Brinsmead brought the doctrine of original sin to the forefront in Adventist theology for the first time. Certainly W. H. Branson gave little evidence of being aware of it in *Our Firm Foundation*. M. L. Andreasen unequivocally asserted that Seventh-day Adventists do not believe in original sin.[7]

Brinsmead had a foundation principle of Reformation theology in the doctrine of original sin. However, at this particular stage in his thinking he could not go all the way with Luther and Calvin because he believed that the solution to original sin had to be in harmony with his traditional Adventist doctrine of the final generation.

Notwithstanding the vitiation of the Reformation's original-sin insight by the doctrine of perfectionism, Brinsmead's message came as good news to many. As with the pre-1950 era, Adventism saw justification as only for the sins of the past, and future salvation was on the basis of inner renewal and character development, albeit by the power of the indwelling Christ. But now Brinsmead was preaching the all-sufficiency of the righteousness of Christ right up to the judgment, and then, by a totally gratuitous act, God would perfect the final generation. With this message (with its obvious affinities to the Reformation gospel), the frank acknowledgment of the continuing presence of sin, and the necessary "charismatic endowments," it is no wonder that the Brinsmead agitation made a considerable impact in the period under discussion.

When we examine the Defense Literature Committee's major

---

6. Alan Starkey, *Basic Brinsmead Belief,* p. 9. Emphasis supplied. Cf. "Firstly, to say that the corrupt principle of sin, the source of evil, the sinful nature, remains in the subconscious life of the believer after his conversion, is *to deny the real nature of the rebirth experience*" (p. 8).

7. "The law of heredity applies to passions and not to pollutions. If pollution is hereditary, then Christ would have been polluted when He came to this world and could not therefore be 'that holy thing.' Luke 1:35. Even the children of an unbelieving husband are called holy, a statement that should be a comfort to the wives of such husbands. I Corinthians 7:14. *As Adventists, however, we do not believe in original sin*" (Andreasen, *Letters to the Churches,* p. 56). Emphasis supplied.

anti-Brinsmead publication of the decade (*The History and Teaching of Robert Brinsmead*), it is clear that the real doctrinal challenge presented by the Awakening was barely dealt with. There is an overwhelming concentration on the alleged personal weakness of the "offshoot leader"[8] and the danger that he and his "dangerous doctrine"[9] constitute for the church. Whereas intense concern and the extravagance of language which often accompanies it are understandable, such an approach undoubtedly did not help the case of the Adventist Church to the degree that a thoughtful concentration on the theological issues might have. The real impact on the Awakening was to come from the new insights of some leading theologians such as Drs. Heppenstall, Ford, and LaRondelle.

The Positive Gains of the 1960's

David McMahon makes a point in the context of Adventism in the 1970's which would seem to be applicable to the second stage of the conflict between church leaders and the Brinsmead agitation in the 1960's:

> All too often theological controversy has been regarded as inimical to revivals and the spiritual prosperity of God's church. But the truth is that it is often when debate and contention are at their height that the Spirit of God descends in power among His people.[10]

The ferment and agitation within Adventism was not all negative. For the first time in the movement's history there appeared a clear challenge to the whole concept of attaining perfection in this life. Dr. Edward Heppenstall, in December of 1963,[11] published an

---

8. Defense Literature Committee, *History and Teaching,* p. 1. Cf. Brinsmead, *Doctrinal Analysis,* p. 1, where Brinsmead cites some 30 or so emotively worded attacks on himself and the Awakening.

9. Defense Literature Committee, *History and Teaching,* p. 37.

10. David McMahon, "Introduction" to Robert D. Brinsmead, *An Answer to "Conflicting Concepts of Righteousness by Faith in the Seventh-day Adventist Church,"* p. vii.

11. Dr. Heppenstall was then Chairman of the Department of Theology at Andrews University.

article entitled "Is Perfection Possible?"[12] The Reformation tone of his approach is obvious:

> It is fatal to believe that if only we could become totally surrendered to Christ, the sinful nature would be eradicated. The law of sin and death continues to operate within us. ...
>
> The basic doctrine of the Christian faith is salvation by grace alone. ...
>
> Salvation by grace alone means that absolute perfection and sinlessness cannot be realized here and now.

Dr. Heppenstall has been fond of viewing the essence of sin as egoism. For him, sinless perfection is "a misleading effort for self-idealization, the exaltation of self,"[13] the "product of self-seeking," and "results in the worship of some aspect of self."[14] Sinless perfection "exerts a deadly effect upon oneself and upon one's relationship to others."[15] It is divisive in relation to the church and is self-destructive.[16]

Heppenstall saw sinless perfection as inimical to the biblical understanding of grace. In a booklet published by the General Conference Ministerial Association as a supplement to *The Ministry*,[17] he wrote:

> The biblical use of the word "grace" is one. Grace is the eternal and free favor of God, manifested toward the guilty and unworthy. Grace is entirely apart from every supposition of human worth and sinless perfection. Grace belongs where human sinfulness exists. It superabounds over human unworthiness as experienced by the saints even after the close of probation. Sinners are the only persons with whom saving grace is concerned. Let us distinguish between grace as an attribute of Christ and grace as a method of salvation made possible by the sacrifice of Christ.

Heppenstall unequivocally asserted the reality of remaining sin

---

12. Edward Heppenstall, "Is Perfection Possible?" *Signs of the Times,* Dec. 1963.

13. Freeman, *Evaluation of Brinsmead Doctrine,* p. 6.

14. Ibid.

15. Ibid., p. 7.

16. Ibid., pp. 8-9.

17. The supplement contained the following essays: Erwin R. Gane, "Christ and Human Perfection"; Edward Heppenstall, "Some Theological Considerations of Perfection"; Robert W. Olson, "Outline Studies on Christian Perfection and Original Sin." Dr. Heppenstall's section is on pages 14-24.

in the believer clear up until the second coming of Christ.[18] Brinsmead was in error because he advocated a perfection that would take place prior to the second advent. Said Heppenstall: "...there will never be a point in Christian living at which the believer may know that he has finally arrived at sinlessness."[19]

It is no exaggeration to say that Heppenstall's refutation of the Brinsmead doctrine is a distinct high point in Adventist theology.[20] There is not its equal either before the contemporary period or after the commencement of 1950. It appears that Heppenstall could discern the logical conclusion of Brinsmead's Reformation emphasis more clearly than Brinsmead himself. For a time, Brinsmead could not see that Heppenstall's denial of perfection was the logical and inevitable conclusion of his own denial of here-and-now perfectionism.

It was not long before Adventist theologians began to publicly embrace Heppenstall's position.[21] In the latter half of the 1960's a steady stream of articles appeared in Adventist literature, denying the possibility of reaching a condition of sinlessness before the second advent of Christ.[22] The object of these articles was the refutation of Brinsmead's doctrine of perfectionism in the

---

18. "The old creature or the old man remains with us until the day of our death or the day of Christ's coming; but as long as we look at Christ the author and the finisher of our faith, sin and self cannot prevail. ... The Christian believes that there still remains in the regenerate man a fountain of evil, that sin always exists in the saints till they are divested of their mortal bodies. ... This original sin remains in Christians and non-Christians until they die or are translated" (Edward Heppenstall, "Definition of Righteousness," in lessons at Andrews University, pp. 18-20). "We find here [1 John 1:8-10] the most solemn warning against the doctrine of sinless perfection in this life. ... The Christian knows that there still remains in him a fountain of evil, a depraved nature" (idem, "Is Perfection Possible?").

19. Freeman, *Evaluation of Brinsmead Doctrine*, p. 8.

20. Once again it needs to be remembered that we are speaking of the degree to which Adventist theology approximates to its avowed Reformation heritage.

21. Theologians such as Dr. Desmond Ford, Prof. Hans K. LaRondelle, Elders Taylor G. Bunch, Ralph S. Watts, L. C. Naden, Harry W. Lowe, Norval F. Pease, and Dr. Raymond F. Cottrell.

22. See Raymond F. Cottrell, *Perfection in Christ* (This statement of Cottrell is by no means the strongest statement of the new Adventist approach.); Harry W. Lowe, *Redeeming Grace*, esp. pp. 117-47 (Lowe is clearer than Cottrell on the refutation of perfection.); E. W. Vick, *Let Me Assure You;* L. C. Naden, *The Perfecting of the Saints;* idem, *In Quest of Holiness;* Defense Literature Committee, *Perfection* (This gives a scriptural use of the word *perfection* and recommends Benjamin B. Warfield's *Perfectionism.).* See also: "Webster defines perfection as being 'blameless' and 'flawless' with characters 'fully formed,' 'completely developed,' 'satisfying the highest expectation,' and having reached 'full maturity.' It is stated that perfectionism from a theological viewpoint is 'the doctrine that a state of freedom from sin is attainable, or has been attained, in the earthly life. ... We

judgment.

We should not fail to notice the interesting turn of events here. In the early years of the decade Brinsmead was opposed because he placed the attainment of perfection too *late*. He was accused of putting off until the judgment what needs to be done *now*. Then there was an about-face, and Brinsmead was attacked for putting the attainment of complete moral perfection too *soon!* He was accused of putting in the judgment what would not take place until after the judgment, at Christ's return.

The sharp break with Adventist tradition should also be noted. The leaders of the church — via the Defense Literature Committee and some leading theologians in the wake of Heppenstall's new theology — swept aside the teaching of over one hundred years of Adventist theology! The impassioned perfectionism of M. L. Andreasen in *The Sanctuary Service* and *The Book of Hebrews*, the perfectionistic emphasis of W. H. Branson, and the implicit perfectionism of *Questions on Doctrine* — all were turned out of Adventism in no uncertain terms by this new theology.

The Awakening supporters at that time were only too aware that such a clear break with traditional Adventism had taken place. In response to Pastor L. C. Naden's *The Perfecting of the Saints*, Brinsmead issued the following challenge:

> I challenge pastor Naden to produce any statement in responsible Seventh-day Adventist literature, written prior to the present Awakening message, which teaches that God's people will not become morally perfect and sinless until Jesus comes in the clouds of heaven. That is simply not basic Adventist doctrine.[23]

It appears that this challenge was never taken up, and this is not surprising. To the knowledge of this writer, it would be impossible to find support for Heppenstall's position in pre-1950 Adventist theology.

---

should remember that only when Jesus comes can we be made perfect" (Taylor G. Bunch, "When Can We Claim Sinless Perfection?" *The Ministry,* Dec. 1965). "We will never reach sinless perfection in this life" (Ralph S. Watts, "God's Crash Program for the Church," *Review and Herald,* 19 May 1966). "The consecrated believer has sin *in* him but no sin *on* him, just as Christ had sin *on* Him but no sin *in* Him. ... every converted soul still has his old nature to fight. ... Our old nature will be finally destroyed at glorification when our Lord returns. Then we will have sin neither in us nor on us" (Desmond Ford, *Signs of the Times,* Australian ed., 1 Aug. 1967).

23. Brinsmead, *Timing of Revelation 18,* p. 37.

What *is* surprising is how Dr. Heppenstall could teach such a doctrine (and apparently lead others to embrace it), yet avoid the condemnation of the church's leaders. What is even more surprising is that the official Defense Literature Committee and the highly regarded *Review and Herald* should espouse the same teaching and have no public answering to do. Reflection on the reception of *Questions on Doctrine* will reveal that it did not enjoy the same privileges as did this new teaching. Certainly Heppenstall and others were advocating no peripheral issue. The doctrine of the perfecting of the final generation stands near the heart of Adventist theology.

The only answer to the above phenomenon that we have been able to arrive at is that the untroubled reception of Heppenstall's anti-perfectionism was an index of the degree to which Adventist leaders saw the Brinsmead challenge as undesirable. On the other hand, those who today see themselves as espousing a faithful Reformation position are inclined to see the situation at the time of Heppenstall's revolution as *providential*. The breakthrough of Heppenstall into a fuller Reformation position may have been impossible if the church had not been fighting the Brinsmead teaching.

The irony of the period must not pass unnoticed. At the time of Heppenstall's revolutionary anti-perfectionism, the Brinsmead "faction" (as Adventist leaders designated it) was more conservatively Adventist than was the church's own Defense Literature Committee. Because the Brinsmead agitation did not wish to cut loose from historic Adventist theology, it passionately resisted the emphasis of Heppenstall. In fact, so preoccupied was the Awakening in preserving what it saw as historic Adventism that the Reformation emphasis of its platform definitely took a subsidiary place in its teaching during the latter half of the 1960's. The Awakening became preoccupied with defending Adventist perfectionism instead of majoring on the Reformation gospel.[24] The irony of the situation within the Brinsmead group was that Heppenstall's stronger Reformation emphasis against perfectionism

24. Almost all of the Awakening literature reveals this fact. Examples are Robert D. Brinsmead's reply to L. C. Naden in ibid. and Dr. Jack Zwemer's defense of the Awakening teaching in Freeman, *Evaluation of Brinsmead Doctrine,* pp. 15-24.

lessened the Awakening's stress on the gospel that it had so force-fully proclaimed in the early years of the decade.

To conclude this aspect of the 1960's, we must draw attention to the positive gains that were made toward the realization of the Advent movement's objective: (1) The reality of original sin became embedded in Adventist theology among such scholars as Heppenstall and Ford. (2) The corollary of this position was a clear repudiation of the possibility of moral perfection in this life—an embracing of the *simul justus et peccator* (at the same time righteous and a sinner) of the Reformers. In these two features there took place a breakthrough into Reformation theology such as had not been seen in the history of the Adventist Church since her inception.

Encouraging Features of the 1960's

A perusal of Seventh-day Adventist literature (especially the *Review and Herald*) in the 1960's indicates that the church was endeavoring to honor her call to be the special heir of the Reformers. There are repeated warnings against legalism as well as numerous statements to the effect that the future of the church lies in the recovery of the true preaching of righteousness by faith. R.S. Watts is typical: "There is no work in our world so great and so glorious, no work that God honors so much, as the gospel of justification in the Lord Jesus."[25]

The same Watts reflects the perspective of the Reformation in his article on "God's Way Is Grace."[26] Unlike *Questions on Doctrine*, his view of grace is not in the Augustinian-Tridentine tradition but that of the Reformation. Grace is not a regenerating power but "the favor and loving kindness on God's part . . . wholly undeserved and unmerited." Watts even makes a brief contrast between his view of grace and that of Roman Catholicism. "Roman Catholicism," he says, "teaches that a man is justified, at least in part, by his own righteousness, infused and inherent, rather than by divine right-

---

25. Ralph S. Watts, "The Message That Brings the Latter Rain," *Review and Herald,* 20 Oct. 1960, p. 10.
26. Ralph S. Watts, "God's Way Is Grace," *Review and Herald,* 30 May 1963, pp. 2-3.

eousness vicarious and imputed." Convincingly, Watts concludes his article with an attack on all human works as contributing to man's salvation in any way.

Watts also directed his attention to the subject of justification and came down solidly in the perspective of the Reformers. Justification unto life eternal is by the imputed righteousness of Christ. Justification does not mean "to make righteous" but rather "to declare righteous." The righteousness by which we attain to everlasting life is what Christ does *for* us and not what he does *in* us.[27]

In the *Review and Herald* of April 21, 1960, Dr. W. G. C. Murdoch also departed from *Questions on Doctrine's* perspective of grace.[28] For Murdoch, grace is God's good will and lovingkindness in the Christ event. Murdoch does not look to the work of the indwelling Christ but to the work of Christ *outside the believer* at Calvary as the meaning and wonder of grace.

One theologian within Adventism in the 1960's who showed a steady reliance upon the perspective of the Reformation was an Australian, Dr. Desmond Ford.[29] In examining the teaching of Ford, it must be said that he showed a praiseworthy consistency in Reformation theology during a period of change. As we have already noted, Ford was explicit in his affirmation of the doctrine of original sin.[30] He taught this consistently through the 1960's and into the 1970's.[31] Ford also strongly repudiated perfectionism as being contrary to the gospel.[32] Likewise, he maintained the Protes-

27. Ralph S. Watts, "The Faith That Saves," *Review and Herald,* 4 June 1963, pp. 1, 4.

28. W. G. C. Murdoch, "The Only Way of Salvation," *Review and Herald,* 21 Apr. 1960, pp. 6, 7.

29. Desmond Ford was Chairman of the Department of Theology at Avondale College, New South Wales, Australia.

30. See n. 22 above.

31. For many years Desmond Ford has written a section of the Australian edition of *Signs of the Times* entitled "Bible Answers." A survey of this section over the years will corroborate what is said in the text of this book concerning Ford. For Ford's views on original sin, depravity, and sinlessness, see Desmond Ford, "Perfect Love," *Signs of the Times,* Australian ed., Mar. 1964; 1 Aug. 1967; idem, "What About Romans 6?" ibid., Oct. 1969; idem, "Some Children Like Saints," ibid., June 1971; idem, "The Case of the Baptist," ibid., June 1971; idem, "Are They Born with Sin?" ibid., Aug. 1971.

32. For Ford's anti-perfectionism perspective and indeed for other clear statements on his conscious stand in the tradition of the Reformation during the 1960's, see Desmond Ford, *Unlocking God's Treasury,* esp. pp. 15-18.

tant view of forensic justification[33] and the Protestant stance on the sinlessness of Christ's human nature.[34] He not only espoused the *gospel* aspect of the Brinsmead teaching of the 1960's (i.e., that Christ is our righteousness in heaven in the hour of the judgment), but he did so along with a clear Reformation perspective on *perfectionism*. Thus, it would not be far from the truth to say that, already in the 1960's, Dr. Ford anticipated the clear Reformation stream that was to emerge within Adventism in the 1970's.

The 1960's witnessed still other indications of the Adventist Church's seeking to remain true to her belief that God had called her to preach the gospel of the Reformation in a way not possible for other Christian bodies. For instance, it was in this decade that H. K. LaRondelle went to the Free University of Amsterdam to study for his doctorate under the Reformed scholar, G. C. Berkouwer. LaRondelle's doctoral dissertation was eventually published under the title, *Perfection and Perfectionism: A Dogmatic-Ethical Study of Biblical Perfection and Phenomenal Perfectionism*. The study stands squarely in the perspective of the Reformation.

At the beginning of this chapter we indicated that the turbulent decade of the 1960's yielded by no means unequivocal support for the Reformation gospel. The same fountain yielded mutually exclusive material. We have reserved other *encouraging* features of the period's theological output until this point in order to provide a contrast with elements *contrary* to the Reformation perspective.

Whereas the Defense Literature Committee of the general Conference was happy (?) to publish the revolutionary theology of Heppenstall on perfectionism, it also published material which

---

33. See Q. 10, "Can a man repent of himself?"; Q. 11, "How only can righteousness be obtained?" ibid., p. 15. See also "Righteousness by Faith" (p. 17). As far back as July, 1959, in response to the question, "What is meant by justification?" Ford unequivocally expressed the Protestant view of justification: "The word 'justification' has a forensic significance. ... it has legal associations and it is vitally connected with issues of law. One definition would be 'The declaring of a person to be righteous according to the law.'. . . Thus when the sinner personally and gratefully accepts Christ's payment of his sins on Calvary, then God imputes to that sinner the righteousness of Christ instead of his own sins. . . . The divine acquittal imputes innocence because of the sinner's acceptance of One who alone has perfect righteousness . . ." (Desmond Ford, *Signs of the Times*, Australian ed., July 1959). Cf. idem, "Grace or Works?" ibid., Jan. 1960.

34. When we come to the decade of the 1970's, we shall have occasion to look more fully at this aspect of Desmond Ford's teaching. For a sample of the 1960's, see Desmond Ford, "Christ's Death," *Signs of the Times*, Australian ed., Sept. 1968; idem, "Did Christ Have Sinful Thoughts?" ibid., Mar. 1969.

was diametrically opposed to his position. The same committee which issued Heppenstall's explicit denial of perfection in this life also issued, in 1967 (some four years *after* Heppenstall's initial public exposition on perfection), *Basic Brinsmead Belief*. Written by Alan Starkey, this publication stated:

> ... to say that the corrupt principle of sin, the source of evil, the sinful nature, remains in the subconscious life of the believer until the final atonement *puts off the work which must be done today.* One woman became horrified when I insisted that sins must be "blotted out" of the life today. She believed that this was the work of the final atonement.[35]

Likewise, in the *Review and Herald* we have both advocation of perfectionism and the denial of perfectionism.[36] There are articles which assert the Protestant forensic nature of justification,[37] and there are others which include the inward work of regeneration in the article of justification.[38] H. L. Rudy is one of the most explicit examples of the latter. Justification "is the coming of the Spirit of Christ into the heart of those who believe that changes their status from 'children of wrath' to 'children of God.'"[39] Yet for Kenneth H. Wood, justification is having the righteousness of Christ put to our account, a legal transaction brought about by God.[40]

It must be said that, in the decade of the 1960's, Adventism's theological output on the gospel comes down in favor of the Roman Catholic perspective to a greater degree than that of the Reformation.[41] Even the more Protestant authors such as R. S. Watts have the tendency to relegate justification to forgiveness of *past sins* only and to see it as having only *initial* significance. As with pre-1950 Adventism, this results in a tendency to subordinate

---

35. Starkey, *Basic Brinsmead Belief,* p. 9. Emphasis supplied. Cf. n. 6 above.

36. See C. J. Ritchie, "Sanctification—Imparted Righteousness," *Review and Herald,* 1 June 1961; L. C. Naden, "Christian Perfection—How Do We Attain It?" ibid., 17 Sept. 1964.

37. E.g., B. A. Scherr, "The Gospel in Romans," *Review and Herald,* 7 Jan. 1960, pp. 9-10.

38. E.g., Watts, "God's Way Is Grace," pp. 2-3.

39. H. L. Rudy, "Adopted into the Heavenly Family," *Review and Herald,* 14 Apr. 1960, pp. 9-10. Cf. the contrary position in "The Faith That Saves," ibid., 6 June 1963, pp. 1, 4-5.

40. Kenneth H. Wood, "The Goal Is Perfection," *Review and Herald,* 30 Nov. 1967, p. 3.

41. For explicit Tridentine theology of the gospel in addition to the above citations, see C. J. Ritchie, "Justified through Imputed Righteousness," *Review and Herald,* 27 Apr. 1961; L. B. Reynolds, "The Mystery Finished," ibid., 28 May 1964, pp. 4-6; E. W. Marter, "The Meaning of the Law in Galatians," ibid., 17 Dec. 1964, pp. 2-3.

justification to sanctification. F. E. Brainard puts it as follows:

> This act of justification is wholly the work of God. ... The newly
> converted man, having been cleansed from guilt, is prepared to
> take the next step toward heaven and eternal life.[42]

E. E. Wheeler can speak of leaning too heavily on the imputed
righteousness of Christ and not seeking to strive so that more and
more righteousness may be imparted in order that we may need
less and less imputed righteousness to cover past sins![43] The subordination of justification to sanctification is expressed again by F.
G. Clifford, who says that if we need to have an understanding of
what Christ has done *for* us, there is an even greater need to let
Him do His effectual work *in* us.[44]

It is obvious that, while there are some encouraging aspects in
Adventism's articulation of the Reformation gospel in the 1960's,
the real theological gains of the decade are to be found in the
affirmation of original sin and the repudiation of perfection in this
life. This significant advance appears in the theology of men such
as Edward Heppenstall, Desmond Ford, and H. K. LaRondelle.

At the Close of the Decade

Let us summarize the decade under discussion. Looked at from one
angle, the 1960's perpetuate pre-1950 Adventism. To a greater or
lesser degree, the Adventist theology of the gospel has always had
two fundamentally conflicting elements — that of Trent and that of
the Reformers. This situation does not change in the 1960's. The
two streams of thought are still present.

However, notwithstanding this unity with pre-1950 Adventism,
there is also distinction. The 1960's was a decade of definite advance in the area of soteriology. Standing on the shoulders of the
Christological advance of the 1950's, there emerged a strong doctrine of original sin and a denial of perfection in the salvation

---

42. F. E. Brainard, "Three Steps to Heaven," *Review and Herald,* 11 Feb. 1960, pp. 6-7.

43. E. E. Wheeler, "Paul — Preacher of Perfection," *Review and Herald,* 6 Aug. 1964, p. 3.

44. F. G. Clifford, "God's Righteousness May Be Ours," *Review and Herald,* 11 Oct. 1962,
pp. 9-11.

process. These aspects were new in Adventist theology.

It is not only that there arose in the 1960's a clearer grasp of what the Reformation gospel meant, but the Protestant message—no doubt due to doctrinal conflict—was brought to the forefront more clearly and forcefully than ever before in the history of Adventism. It was a period in which the Reformation gospel was gaining ground in Adventist consciousness.

Finally, the 1960's was an era in which Adventism was seen more clearly than ever before to be lacking unity on the central area of its theology. To illustrate this, we refer again to the church's opposition to Brinsmead's teaching. The Awakening was opposed (1) on the basis of a strong belief in here-and-now perfection. But it was also opposed (2) on the basis of a strong denial of perfection in this life. What was the "official" position of the denomination on this issue? The only answer can be that official Adventism adopted *both* positions.

The fact that official Adventism sought to publicly adopt both positions throws an interesting light on the situation in the 1960's. The fact is that *both* official Adventism and Brinsmead contained conflicting elements in their systems. Brinsmead was seeking to effect a synthesis between Reformation justification by faith alone and traditional Adventist belief in perfection. Official Adventism was holding, on the one hand, to a here-and-now perfection based on traditional Adventist reliance upon the perspective of Trent and, on the other hand, to a radical denial of perfection with its roots in Reformation theology and the Christological advance of *Questions on Doctrine*.

The decade of the 1960's closes with conflict between official Adventism and the Brinsmead group. But there is also conflict within the respective positions. It remains to the next decade to see how these conflicts are resolved and how the gospel of the Reformers fares in that resolution.

7

Advance and Retreat: The 1970's

The 1970's is the period when, for the first time, two consistent streams of thought on the gospel emerge in Adventism. One stream carries the Christological gains of the 1950's and the soteriological gains of the 1960's to their logical end. The other stream retreats from those gains into pre-1950 Adventism. This division brings Adventism to the threshold of an unprecedented shaking. It is now our task to trace the steps of this astounding development.

Brinsmead Capitulates to Heppenstall and Ford

At the beginning of 1970, Robert Brinsmead and his colleagues became deeply involved in studying the issues of the Protestant Reformation and the implications of Pauline theology. In the study of Reformation theology and Roman Catholic theology, Brinsmead came to a renewed understanding of the issues of the sixteenth century—in particular, *the meaning and implications of justification by faith alone.*

The rediscovery of the Reformation gospel brought about a revolution in Brinsmead's thinking.[1] He understood for the first time the real meaning of justification by faith alone—its primacy, centrality, and all-sufficiency. It became clear to him what Luther meant in calling justification the article of the standing and falling church.

What this meant for Brinsmead and his colleagues was that, whereas in the past the Reformation had always been viewed in the light of the distinctive Adventist perspective, now the Adventist perspective had to be viewed in the light of the Reformation. Brinsmead came to believe that any *building* upon the Reformation had to be a building *upon* the Reformation and not *in place of* the Reformation. Whatever contribution Adventism had to give to the world, that contribution must not conflict with the central article of Reformation theology—the gospel of justification by faith alone.

Theologically, Brinsmead's rediscovery meant the following:

1. Brinsmead was forced to accept the position of Heppenstall, Ford, and others on the question of perfection. Although he had taught a *modified* perfectionism (i.e., perfection in the judgment but not before), Brinsmead now came to realize that even such a modified perfectionism and justification by faith alone cannot live in the same house happily. Niebuhr focused the issue for him: righteousness for the Reformers was a *faith*-righteousness, and they saw their true nature and destiny in terms of this righteousness and not in any tangible, empirical righteousness in the historical process. Heppenstall and Ford were right: there can be no perfection until Christ returns.

2. Using the Reformation gospel as a canon, Brinsmead and his colleagues came to the conclusion that the traditional Adventist way of treating "righteousness by faith" was in harmony with Roman Catholic theology and not with that of the Reformers. As we have had ample occasion to note, traditional Adventism saw justification as initial forgiveness for sins of the past, while regeneration and sanctification were viewed as qualifying a person to stand in the coming judgment. Righteousness by faith was thought

---

1. See Brinsmead, *Review of the Awakening Message,* pts. 1-2.

to encompass both justification *and* sanctification. Brinsmead came to the conviction—via Luther and Calvin (and Chemnitz)—that righteousness by faith means *justification only*. He saw that to continue in the thought patterns of traditional Adventism was to mingle law and gospel, to depend ultimately upon character development and inner renewal rather than upon an alien righteousness for our acceptance with God, and to be forced into positing perfectionism in this life. He concluded that the traditional Adventist sense of "righteousness by faith" leads to a focusing on the saint—the dreadful turning in upon ourselves.

3. Justification by faith alone in the alien righteousness of Christ called Brinsmead's traditional Adventist eschatology into question. In his theology of the 1960's he had sought to keep original sin and in-the-judgment perfectionism under one roof. Now the gospel of Paul and the Reformers made it clear that his in-the-judgment perfectionism was an attempt to deal with original sin in a way which amounted to competition with the active and passive obedience of the God-man Substitute. Brinsmead's in-the-judgment perfectionism was an emergency measure to handle the original-sin problem. But the gospel of the Reformers taught him that justification by faith in the merits of Christ was the only effectual method of dealing with original sin.[2] Whereas in traditional Adventism the *initial, mere* nature of justification was a concession to final acceptance on the basis of inner renewal, Brinsmead's final renewal was a concession to justification, yet also a vitiation of it.[3] According to him, all this "had to go." Justification was seen to be clearly eschatological. It was God's *final* judgment-day verdict received here and now by faith.

For Brinsmead, this eschatological view of justification meant that it can never be subordinated to sanctification, contrary to much traditional Adventist theology. While the believer stands on justification, yet justification is always that to which he is moving. Like the psalmist, the believer can look forward not so much to a

---

2. Brinsmead was impressed with the following quotation: "Justification by faith is really the only answer to the moral perplexities of the doctrine of original sin" (W. H. Griffith Thomas, *The Principles of Theology*, p. 193).

3. In his earlier sanctuary teaching, Brinsmead would speak of justification as being the "outer court," sanctification the "holy place," and perfection the "most holy place."

judgment *of* him by the Judge, but to a judgment *for* him. The judgment is vindication—a vindication that the believer already enjoys by faith.

4. Brinsmead testifies that this rediscovery turned himself and his colleagues outside of themselves to others. With the coming of the gospel of Paul and the Reformers, sectarian mentality began to fade away. Brinsmead sought the fellowship of God's people wherever they could be found. Also, he and his fellow agitators approached their estranged Adventist fellow Christians to confess their errors and seek reconciliation.[4]

The major expression of Brinsmead's new look outward was his publishing venture, *Present Truth* magazine. The fundamental aim of *Present Truth* was to remind Protestants of their Reformation heritage and of how far they had wandered from it.

Brinsmead's Capitulation: A More Dangerous Threat

The reader will not fail to notice the irony in the above subheading. During the conflict of the 1960's, church leaders turned to Heppenstall and Ford for an answer to Brinsmead's teachings. Thus, when he capitulated to Heppenstall and Ford's position, one would naturally have expected the leadership to be delighted. However, an almost unbelievable turn of events was to take place: Brinsmead came to be looked upon as a greater threat than ever!

Within Adventism in general, opinion regarding *Present Truth* differed. Avondale's Dr. Desmond Ford and retired Australasian Division President, L. C. Naden, saw Brinsmead's new move to be in the right theological direction. In some respects it was a vindication of Ford and Naden's position on perfection. However, alarm at Brinsmead's "one-sided" view of justification by faith issued from church headquarters in Washington, D.C., where Kenneth Wood and Herbert Douglass, editors of the *Review and Herald*, began to emphasize such things as victory-life piety, the development of sinless-demonstration people in the last generation, the example

---

4. See Brinsmead, *Review of the Awakening Message*, pts. 1-2.

of Christ in sinless living, and the sinful human nature of Christ.

Leading theologians in the church's Australasian Division began to be alarmed at the perfectionistic emphasis of the *Review and Herald* and the undoing of the Christological gains of *Questions on Doctrine* in the 1950's. And in North America, Dr. Heppenstall as well as some leading theologians at Andrews University were also unhappy with the perfectionism of the *Review and Herald* and its teaching on the sinful human nature of Christ.

Polarization Becomes Obvious

If there was any doubt about whether church leaders were taking an opposite stance toward the new Brinsmead message, such doubt was dispelled in 1974 with the appearance of a special issue of the *Review and Herald* on the topic of "Righteousness by Faith."[5] It was diametrically opposed to Brinsmead's teaching. The special issue defined righteousness by faith as

> ... more than a doctrine, it is a relationship with a purpose. And if we turn our backs on sin, and let Christ live His life within us, it doesn't matter what we call the process.[6]

It seems that *Present Truth* magazine was being criticized for being cerebral in its approach to the gospel because it spoke much of the "doctrine" of righteousness by faith.

In the same special issue, Don Neufeld describes righteousness by faith as an "experience,"[7] and the "no condemnation" of Romans 8 is interpreted in the way of Trent.[8] C. Mervyn Maxwell says unequivocally, "Righteousness by faith is much more than forgiveness of sin; it is also victory over sin."[9] Other passages could be cited to show that the *Review and Herald* persists in the traditional Adventist definition of righteousness by faith as including both

---

5. Undated but issued 16 May 1974.

6. George E. Vandeman, "Meet the Master," *Review and Herald,* special issue, "Righteousness by Faith" [16 May 1974], p. 3.

7. Don F. Neufeld, "Righteousness by Faith — Is It Biblical?" *Review and Herald,* special issue, "Righteousness by Faith" [16 May 1974], p. 6.

8. Ibid., p. 8.

9. C. Mervyn Maxwell, "Christ and Minneapolis 1888," *Review and Herald,* special issue, "Righteousness by Faith" [16 May 1974], p. 18.

justification and sanctification.[10] Looked at from an academic perspective, it is no exaggeration to say that this special issue *majors* on sanctification and character development and a hagiocentric (believer-centered) emphasis.[11]

Herbert Douglass has emerged in the 1970's as the one who is seeking to make the Andreasen-Branson perfectionism dominant in Adventist thinking. In the special issue of the *Review and Herald,* he proposes to tell his reading audience "Why God Is Urgent and Yet Waits." The answer is: "God waits for a people who will prove that what Jesus did ... could be done by His followers. ..."[12] "For such a people," says Douglass, "God waits."[13] This is the here-and-now perfectionism of the early (and later) years of the 1960's, and it characterizes the *Review and Herald* stand of the church in the period of the 1970's.

A few weeks after the distribution of the *Review and Herald* special issue in Australia, Brinsmead issued a brochure entitled *A Statement to My S.D.A. Friends.*[14] Without mentioning the *Review and Herald,* he called into question the assumption that sanctification belongs to the Pauline article of righteousness by faith. Brinsmead claimed that righteousness by faith is nothing done by us or felt by us and is never a quality in us. The righteousness in "*righteousness* by faith" is the doing and dying of Christ, which is ours by faith in the merciful verdict of God. Brinsmead declared that this position is faithful to that of the sixteenth-century Reformers and all those Protestants who have stood with them for some four hundred years. To call sanctification "righteousness by faith" is to side with the Council of Trent against the Protestant Reformation.

If the special issue of the *Review and Herald* represents the position of church leaders—and subsequent events show that it

---

10. Herbert E. Douglass, "Why God Is Urgent and Yet Waits," *Review and Herald,* special issue, "Righteousness by Faith" [16 May 1974], p. 23. Kenneth H. Wood, "Jesus Made the Way Plain in Parables," ibid., p. 24. Here Wood says that righteousness by faith "is a supernatural change."

11. See esp. Vandeman's article cited in n. 6 above.

12. Douglass, "Righteousness by Faith," p. 22.

13. Ibid., p. 23.

14. The subtitle reads, *Is Sanctification the Same As Righteousness by Faith? Rome Says Yes; The Reformation Says No; Where Do Seventh-day Adventists Stand?*

Ford was confident that this was the predominant concession at Palmdale, and he said it was a "first" in the history of Seventh-day Adventism.[24]

Quite a debate followed in Australia, although many church members were unaware of its controversial background. This conflict and polarization were viewed from very different perspectives. As Ray Martin's *Objective Digest Report* (1976) observed:

> Some see it [Ford's doctrine] as the destruction of all that Adventism has stood for and as the omega of apostasy, while others see it as the beginning of that truth which will lighten the earth with the glory of God and believe that at last Adventism has come of age.

As time went on, it began to be obvious that some influential *Review and Herald* leaders did not accept Ford's position on the definition of righteousness by faith. Both the editor of the *Review and Herald,* Kenneth H. Wood, and the President of the General Conference, Robert H. Pierson, made their position clear. Wood quotes the *Seventh-day Adventist Encyclopedia,* which says that righteousness by faith includes *both* justification and sanctification,[25] and then goes on to say: "The Palmdale statement concurs with this view."[26] Further on he continues:

> We think it only fair to say... that those who hold sanctification to be a part of "righteousness by faith" seem to place greater emphasis on holy living than do those who exclude it; also, they seem to give greater emphasis to humanity's part in cooperating with divinity in the plan of salvation. This is perhaps because they consider the gospel not merely as the good news that through Christ repentant souls may have a new standing before God, but that through Him sinners may be transformed.[27]

In subsequent articles on the Palmdale statement,[28] Wood makes clear how he understands the gospel. He writes:

---

24. "And it's a wonderful thing that recently in America we could make a statement like this for the first time in our history, a wonderful thing" (Desmond Ford, Avondale College Chapel address, 18 May 1976).

25. *Seventh-day Adventist Encyclopedia,* p. 1085.

26. Kenneth H. Wood, "F. Y. I. [For Your Information]," pt. 1, *Review and Herald,* 21 Oct. 1976, p. 2. Notice that Palmdale spoke of "the *experience* of justification by faith."

27. Ibid.

28. Wood, "F. Y. I.," pts. 2-4, *Review and Herald,* 28 Oct. 1976, pp. 2, 19; 4 Nov. 1976, pp. 2, 15; 18 Nov. 1976, pp. 2, 13. Cf. Kenneth H. Wood, "Fit for a Wedding," ibid., 2 Dec. 1976, pp. 2, 11.

We think it is important to understand that the gospel (good news) is not merely an announcement of what Christ has done in the past to save a lost world, it is an announcement of what Christ wants to do, and is able to do, in the present. It is not merely an announcement of Bethlehem and Calvary, it is an announcement of a living Saviour, a Saviour who is able to save to the uttermost (Heb. 7:25), a Saviour who can save not merely from the penalty of sin but from the power of sin (Titus 2:11-14), a Saviour who not only forgives but cleanses from sin (1 John 1:9), a Saviour who is able to keep us from yielding to temptation (Jude 24), a Saviour who ministers on our behalf in the heavenly sanctuary (Heb. 8:1, 2).[29]

The President of the General Conference, Robert H. Pierson, gives his influential contribution in an article entitled "What Is Righteousness by Faith?"[30] Pierson follows Wood in referring to the Adventist *Encyclopedia* and then says:

From these words it is clear that the Seventh-day Adventist Church accepts the two phases or steps in the experience of righteousness by faith. One is the "instantaneous experience," known as justification, ... [which is] the imputed righteousness of Jesus ... and the resultant peace and joy in Christ. ...
    The second phase is a "lifelong experience of Christian living". ...[31]

At least two things became clear after Palmdale: (1) The Palmdale statement settled nothing. Despite its preamble, which confesses that Adventism has for years lacked a clear statement on righteousness by faith, the statement itself perpetuates rather than corrects that situation. (2) Brinsmead's contribution to Ford's theology became evident. As we have already noted, the idea that Ford has become a follower of Brinsmead is too broad an assertion for the evidence to support. It would be just as true to say that Brinsmead has become a follower of Ford. What has become clear after Palmdale is the precise way in which Brinsmead did influence Ford. Brinsmead, via *Present Truth* magazine, caused Ford to sharpen his definition of righteousness by faith into the shape of

---

29. Wood, "F. Y. I.," pt. 3, p. 2.

30. Robert H. Pierson, "What Is Righteousness by Faith?" *The Ministry,* Feb. 1977, p. 9.

31. Ibid. It is noteworthy that Pierson includes the subjective aspect, "the resultant peace and joy in Christ," in his definition of *justification* as the first phase of righteousness by faith.

the biblical-Reformation understanding of it as *justification alone*. Brinsmead taught Ford to view the Adventist concept of righteousness by faith in the light of the Reformation, and not the Reformation position in the light of Adventist usage. What this meant for Ford was that he not only came to see the righteousness of faith as meaning justification alone, but he also came to see the all-determining significance of justification by faith for life and doctrine.[32] His whole perspective was sharpened more than fundamentally altered by encounter with *Present Truth*.

Palmdale added fuel to the fire of controversy within Adventism over the biblical-Reformation significance of righteousness by faith. Many who had not previously been aware of the division joined ranks according to their convictions.

This controversy reached a new level of tension in the publication of the Adult Sabbath School Lessons for April-May-June, 1977, entitled *Jesus, the Model Man*.[33] If there were ever any doubts in the minds of some Adventists as to where the American leadership of the 1970's stands in relation to *Questions on Doctrine* and the soteriological gains of the 1960's, this Lesson Quarterly dispelled those doubts once and for all.

In the Quarterly, Herbert Douglass presents the idea that the Second Person of the Godhead divested Himself of His divine powers and prerogatives.[34] "Our Model is not merely an example which beckons us on but is never to be reached."[35] Jesus was altogether human and possessed a sinful nature common to all men. Hence, Jesus is qualified to be our Example, and the gospel (good news) is that He has proved we can overcome sin and live exactly (sinlessly) as He did.[36]

The Lesson Quarterly caused no small stir in Adventist circles.

---

32. For Brinsmead's emphasis on this point, see Robert D. Brinsmead, "St. Paul's Message of Justification," *Present Truth*, Apr. 1972, pp. 5-10; idem, "The Righteousness Which Is of Faith," ibid., special issue, "Justification by Faith" [May 1972], pp. 14-17; idem, "The Radical Meaning of *Sola Fide*," ibid., June 1975, pp. 6-7. Cf. idem, *Statement;* idem, *The Current Righteousness by Faith Dialogue*. In *Current Dialogue*, Brinsmead gives 10 reasons why sanctification cannot be included in the article of righteousness by faith.

33. Herbert E. Douglass, *Jesus, the Model Man*. These lessons are used simultaneously by Adventist churches worldwide.

34. Ibid., p. 22.

35. Ibid., p. 96.

36. Ibid.

M. G. Townend (the Sabbath School Director for the Australasian Division) sent a letter to President Pierson and was informed, among other things, that "I [Pierson] have personally gone through the lessons within the last few days, and I received a blessing from the thoughts presented."[37]

As is the custom, the Quarterly was sent to scholars and theologians for perusal before its final draft. The leading theologians of the Australasian Division were deeply apprehensive and sought to have its publication halted. However, the President of the General Conference informed the Australian leaders that to withdraw the material at that particular stage would only aggravate the situation into a worse state.

The Lesson Quarterly was finally sent out to the local Adventist churches throughout the world, and objections to it followed from ministers, theologians, and laity. Typical is an open letter "To My Fellow Ministers," by Victor P. Kluzit,[38] and the tape-recorded discussion of the Quarterly by Dr. Richard Neis, who expresses fears of heresy.[39] Kluzit calls upon the leaders to repent, and Dr. Neis wonders if some of Douglass' views on Christ "border on blasphemy." An Australian pastor, Max Hatton, calls the Lesson Quarterly "not truly Protestant" and deplores its shallow view of sin.[40]

There is obvious confusion in the minds of many rank-and-file members of the church, and serious division over the very nature and meaning of the gospel exists among Adventist ministers and theologians. There is also confusion over the relation between much teaching in the 1970's[41] and respected works published in the

37. Quoted in M. G. Townend letter to division officers, dated Jan. 24, 1977.

38. Victor P. Kluzit, *An Appeal to Withdraw and Make a Public Confession for the Sabbath School Quarterly Entitled "Jesus, the Model Man" April-June, 1977 (Lev. 26:40, 42).* Kluzit's last paragraph conveys the spirit of his appeal: "Brethren, as an ordained minister of the Seventh-day Adventist church, I have written this protest, for it is necessary for another Joseph to stand today and speak (Luke 20:50, 51) for the Truth that is in Jesus to the Council of Spiritual Shepherds ... and to voice the deepest disapproval to the Laodicean indifference that we have for the One knocking at the door of our church. ... Therefore, This Sabbath School Quarterly has to be withdrawn and public confession made by the General Conference for this denial of Christ. ..."

39. Richard Neis, "Jesus, the Model Man."

40. Max Hatton, *Jesus Our Example,* pp. 2, 8.

41. E.g., the 1970's have seen an unprecedented flood of teaching on perfectionism in Seventh-day Adventism. There is increasing emphasis along the lines of Douglass' Lesson

earlier decades of contemporary Adventism—works such as *Questions on Doctrine*.

Breaking the Synthesis

Prior to 1970, Adventism's view of the gospel was a *synthesis* of Protestant and Roman Catholic elements. It was this synthesis which bound all Adventist theologians together in their articulation of the gospel. The synthesis was to be found even in those theologians who stood closer to the Reformation perspective (e.g., Heppenstall, Ford, and LaRondelle).

When justification and sanctification are synthesized (as in the Council of Trent), sanctification inevitably swallows up justification. Hence, prior to the 1970's—and for those who persist in the synthesis after 1970—*sanctification becomes the predominant emphasis over justification*.

This synthesis of righteousness by faith and sanctification was the weak spot in the theological "attack" of Heppenstall, Ford, and LaRondelle against Brinsmead during the 1960's.[42] Though these theologians took a strong anti-perfectionism position against Brinsmead's teaching, the fact that they still synthesized justification and sanctification in their understanding of righteousness by faith vitiated their anti-perfectionism emphasis. Especially was this so when we consider that Brinsmead could call upon Adventist tradition to support his perfectionism. So long as he saw the gospel as including in its essence the sanctification of the believer and then reflected upon this emphasis in Adventist history, he could not

Quarterly, *Jesus, the Model Man.* See Herbert E. Douglass and Leo R. Van Dolson, *Jesus, the Benchmark of Humanity.*

42. In a paper entitled "Fitness for Heaven: A Dialogue with Robert Brinsmead on Bible Perfection," Hans K. LaRondelle argues that *justification* means "the transformation of the sin-governed heart" (p. 7), "the outpouring of love in the heart that believes" (p. 12), "the impartation of the recreating Holy Spirit" (p. 13). "Bible justification means much more than a mere forensic or legal forgiveness of sin" (p. 14). Instead of the believer's escaping condemnation by virtue of what Christ did on the cross, LaRondelle says, "... when the corrupt channel or nature is made ineffective by the grace of the indwelling Christ, there is no condemnation for the perfected soul. (Rom. 8:1)" (p. 80). LaRondelle came out strongly against perfectionism only after he did his doctoral thesis, *Perfection and Perfectionism,* under G. C. Berkouwer in 1969-70. This thesis contradicts some of LaRondelle's earlier theology.

be moved from his belief of perfection in this life.

This observation is endorsed by the events of the 1970's. Ford appears to have learned the lesson of the 1960's and has come forth with a clear distinction between righteousness by faith and sanctification.[43] However, Heppenstall and LaRondelle have yet to make it clear that they too have broken the synthesis.[44] Thus, it is not surprising that their anti-perfectionism arguments are lacking the leverage needed to pry their fellow Adventists off the notion that there will be a final generation who, because of their sinlessness, will not need the Mediator's benefits.[45]

The *new* element in Adventism's approach to the gospel in the 1970's is the breaking of the synthesis of righteousness by faith and sanctification in the understanding of righteousness by faith. This is the first time in Adventist teaching that the break has taken

---

43. On Oct. 2, 1976, Dr. Ford remarked, "I have used (as many of the brethren have) the expression 'righteousness by faith' to include sanctification" (Desmond Ford, "An Answer to Dr. Russell Standish," sermon transcript, p. 41).

44. In the case of Dr. Hans K. LaRondelle, this synthesis between justification and sanctification is still present after 1970. See Hans K. LaRondelle, "Seventh-day Adventist Statement on Righteousness by Faith." Here LaRondelle says that justification is "a judicial transaction of Christ as heavenly Mediator, but it is more than that. It implies the sanctifying impartation of the Holy Spirit of divine love within the heart of the justified believer (Rom. 5:1, 5; 8:14-16), or stated differently, the indwelling of Christ in the believer's heart (Gal. 2:20; Eph. 3:14-19)" (p. 2). Also: ". . . it can be said that justification sets the repentant believer free from the guilt of sin and delivers him at the same time from the bondage and defiling power of sin" (p. 3). See also idem, "Kommentar van dr. h. k. la rondelle op het artikel van paxton in jeugd, november, 1976" [Commentary of Dr. H. K. LaRondelle on the Article of Paxton in *Youth,* November, 1976]. Here LaRondelle says: "John . . . proclaims the gospel in terms of love to one another. . . ." The "gospel in all its fullness [is] presented to us in the Old Testament" (p. 10 in Dutch original). LaRondelle seems to regard any attempt to clearly *distinguish* between justification and sanctification as a *separation* of the two. But Heppenstall clearly reflects the breaking of the synthesis when he says: "When Paul speaks of righteousness which is by faith, he is not thinking in terms of righteousness in man, but of their legal standing before God. . . . 'Justify' never means in Scripture to pour the quality of righteousness into someone, but to establish righteousness forensically, or to make righteous by an act which is entirely outside man" (Edward Heppenstall, "The Meaning of Righteousness," in lessons at Andrews University, pp. 39-40). It here seems that Heppenstall is the forerunner of the Ford-Brinsmead theology. It only remains for him to indicate that he consistently carries through with this understanding of righteousness by faith. It seems that LaRondelle, if he is consistent with himself at his best (i.e., in his thesis, *Perfection and Perfectionism),* must also come out on the side of Reformation theology.

45. The "dialogue" of Heppenstall and LaRondelle with the perfectionists over the possibility of perfection in this life may be seen in Herbert E. Douglass, Edward Heppenstall, Hans K. LaRondelle, and C. Mervyn Maxwell, *Perfection: The Impossible Possibility.*

place.[46] Where it has occurred, there is an unashamed return to the gospel of the Reformation.

Since 1970, Brinsmead has never ceased to stress the all-sufficiency of justification and to deliver attacks on anything that would in any way downgrade this article of the Christian faith.[47] For both Brinsmead and Ford, the centrality of justification lies at the heart of the gospel of Paul and the Reformers. Yet in the face of Brinsmead and Ford's breaking of the synthesis between righteousness by faith and sanctification, there is now a definite effort by others to maintain it.

Adventism Today

It is now our purpose to examine the place of the Reformation gospel in Adventism at the point of the movement's latest development. We have seen that, prior to 1950, Adventist theology of the gospel tended to relegate justification to the status of *mere. Justification was seen as only for the sins of the past.* But what about Adventism today?

The President of the General Conference of Seventh-day Adventists, Elder Robert H. Pierson, quotes approvingly the *Signs of the Times* of 1874 which says: "We are dependent on Christ, first for justification from our past offenses, and, secondly, for grace whereby to render acceptable obedience to His holy law in time to come."[48]

The tendency *to subordinate justification to sanctification* receives its strongest representation in the special issue of the *Re-*

---

46. As the theology of those who have broken the synthesis makes clear, this does not mean a *separation* of justification and sanctification. Rather, the "breaking" means (1) the clear *distinction* between justification and sanctification and (2) the *primacy* of justification. See Desmond Ford, "The Scope and Limits of the Pauline Expression 'Righteousness by Faith,'" in Jack D. Walker, ed., *Documents from the Palmdale Conference on Righteousness by Faith,* pp. 1-13.

47. A sample of Brinsmead's teaching on this point may be seen in Robert D. Brinsmead, *Present Truth,* special issue, "Justification by Faith and the Charismatic Movement" [Sept.-Oct. 1972]; idem, "Justification by Faith and the Current Religious Scene," ibid., Aug. 1973, pp. 14-34; idem, ibid., special issue, "Sanctification," Feb. 1975; idem, "Radical Meaning," pp. 6-7.

48. Quoted in Pierson, "What Is Righteousness by Faith?" p. 9.

view and Herald on "Righteousness by Faith," which, as we have already mentioned, was published by those who wanted to counteract the new-face Brinsmead of the 1970's.[49]

Also, in "Why You Lose What You Don't Use," J. W. McFarland and J. R. Spangler, in contrasting justification and sanctification, have this to say:

> *Justification* blots out the black picture of the *past, sanctification* paints a bright picture for *now* and the *future*; *justification clears* the record, *sanctification keeps* the record clear. ...
> Sanctification as well as justification, is Christ *taking action* in my life.[50]

Though this downgrading of justification is shared by *Review and Herald* editor, Kenneth H. Wood,[51] as well as by George McCready Price,[52] none of these presentations is as explicit as that of Don Hawley in his book, *Getting It All Together*. Hawley says:

> Sanctification then is growing up into Christ; becoming more and more like Him through the *impartation* (actual receiving) of His righteousness. With the passage of time we should require less emphasis on Christ's imputed righteousness and should actually possess more and more of His imparted righteousness.[53]

Arnold V. Wallenkampf, in the *Review and Herald* article, "Saved Solely by Grace," says that "keeping grace" is superior to "forgiving grace" and that we should reach a place where we are able to live without forgiving grace![54]

In our chapter on the gospel of the Reformation, we have seen that such a severe subordination of justification in the interest of sanctification is foreign to the thinking of the Reformers.[55] The

---

49. At least 90% of the special issue of the *Review and Herald* on "Righteousness by Faith" is given over to sanctification. Justification is damned with faint praise.

50. J. W. McFarland and J. R. Spangler, "Why You Lose What You Don't Use," *Century 21: Institute for Better Living,* p. 15. Emphases in original.

51. See Wood, "Fit for a Wedding," pp. 2, 11.

52. "We hear much about receiving Christ's righteousness, but this almost always refers to the *imputation* of this righteousness. This is highly important as a beginning, but there is a much higher stage of attainment, when Christ's righteous character becomes *imparted* to us ..." (George McCready Price, *Review and Herald,* 1 Jan. 1976).

53. Don Hawley, *Getting It All Together,* p. 35. Emphasis in original.

54. Arnold V. Wallenkampf, "Saved Solely by Grace," *Review and Herald,* 9 Sept. 1971, p. 4.

55. See chap. 2, "The Heart of the Reformation."

Avondale Professor of Theology, Dr. Desmond Ford, is aware of this. In the papers he presented at the Palmdale conference, he included an appendix to indicate the "Atlas" nature of justification.[56] Likewise, in *The Soteriological Implications of the Human Nature of Christ*, Ford makes it clear that justification is the *basis* of the believer's holy life and that the Christian's eyes are to be focused on that fact.[57]

In pre-1950 Adventism we encountered an understanding of justification as being the creative action of God *in the life of the believer*. Whereas it is not improper to speak of justification as the *creative* action of God, we have shown that this refers to the believer *in Christ* and not to the believer *in himself*.[58] The same tendency that was found in pre-1950 Adventism is also present in contemporary Adventism: the idea that *justification is the making of the believer to be ontologically righteous in himself*.

Clifford and Standish are explicit. Justification is an inward work involving a change in the character of the person justified.[59] For Dr. Ford, however, "Justification is a declaring righteous, not a making righteous."[60]

Pastor J.W. Lehman of the Campus Hill Church in Loma Linda, California, is in agreement with the Council of Trent in his understanding of justification. In a series of four recorded studies on the theme, "What Is Righteousness?" (1975), he says that righteousness is love, and the believer becomes righteous by having Christ's love poured into his heart. (This emphasis of Lehman is the more interesting since in the same series he delivers forthright attacks upon Pelagianism and semi-Pelagianism.) Further, in his Campus Hill Sabbath Service address called "The Other Half of Forgiveness,"[61] Pastor Lehman deals with "some of the misunder-

---

56. Ford, "Scope and Limits," in Walker, *Documents from Palmdale,* pp. 11-13. The appendix is actually J. I. Packer's "Introduction" to James Buchanan's *The Doctrine of Justification.*

57. Mrs. Desmond Ford, *The Soteriological Implications of the Human Nature of Christ,* pp. 9-10.

58. See chap. 1, appendix, "1888: A Thorn in the Church's Flesh."

59. Clifford and Standish, *Conflicting Concepts,* pp. 24, 53, 56.

60. Desmond Ford, *Redemption, Objective and Subjective,* p. 2.

61. J. W. Lehman, "The Other Half of Forgiveness," transcript of a sermon delivered in the Campus Hill Seventh-day Adventist Church, Loma Linda, Calif., May 10, 1975. This is a major Adventist church in a major Adventist center.

standings and problems of justification by faith." He says: "Thus
far we have been emphasizing that justification by faith is a twofold operation—forgiveness for sin and making us righteous."[62]
The Vice-President of the General Conference, Neal C. Wilson,
endorsed Lehman's perspective in a circulated brochure advertis-
ing his recorded studies.[63]

The Roman Catholic understanding of justification is given
clearest expression in a paper by Erwin R. Gane entitled "Is There
Power in Justification?" He says, "Far from being merely a forensic
act of God, justification involves the most direct and transforming
divine intervention in the life of the Christian believer."[64] The
righteousness of the believer is an *alien* righteousness, says Gane,
because it comes from *without*.[65] But once it is bestowed, it becomes
the property of the believer as well as of Christ.[66] This infused
righteousness immediately qualifies the believer for heaven. Gane
equates the infusion of righteousness with the new birth of John
3:5, and he calls upon the passage in Titus 3:5-6 to support his case.
This new life-righteousness belongs to the believer only so long as
he "allows Jesus to reign."[67] Gane concludes his article by stating
that E. J. Waggoner of 1888 fame taught that justification is the
work of the Spirit in the heart of the believer and that A. G.
Daniells, who intended to revive the 1888 message, saw justification as "a vital experience to be entered into."[68]

This type of approach to the meaning of justification is quite
widespread in contemporary Adventism.[69] From this approach to
the meaning of justification it is only a short step to the idea that

---

62. Ibid. Cf. "Pardon includes not only the removal of condemnation, but also the making
us righteous" (p. 4).

63. *A Gift for Pastors of Seventh-day Adventist Churches in North America* (1 Sept. 1975).
Wilson gave his approval in a personally written letter of Aug. 5, 1975, entitled, "Memo
from Neal C. Wilson, Vice President, North American Division," which was sent out with
the brochure. Lehman says that the righteousness of Rom. 3:21 is the *infused* righteousness of *love*.

64. Erwin R. Gane, "Is There Power in Justification?" p. 1.

65. Ibid., p. 2.

66. Ibid.

67. Ibid., p. 3.

68. Ibid., p. 7.

69. See LaRondelle, "Statement on Righteousness by Faith," p. 2; idem, "The Everlasting
Gospel and Righteousness by Faith," p. 21, in Biblical Research Committee, *North American Bible Conference, 1974.* Here LaRondelle says that Paul guards against a mere

acceptance in the final judgment is on the basis of character renewal. If it be admitted that justification puts us right with God (which Adventism has always believed) and that justification either *includes* or *is* "the grace of sanctification," then it follows that *acceptance must be on the basis of inner renewal.*

In preparation for this book, this author conducted an extensive survey in the United States in 1976 on the topic of justification by faith and the seminary student. Eleven schools were surveyed with a multiple-choice questionnaire. Question six was:

> My acceptance in the final judgment will be based upon
>   (a) my character.
>   (b) the character which Christ has worked out within me.
>   (c) the forgiveness of sins.

Sixty-six percent of the Seventh-day Adventist Andrews University Seminary students who filled out the questionnaire answered with (b): "the character which Christ has worked out within me."

It is not difficult to understand this response of Seventh-day Adventist seminary students when the editor of one of the church's leading papers writes as follows:

> All of us face the final judgment, when God, the Ancient of Days, will sit at the bar of eternal justice, and all who have ever lived will be summoned to appear before Him. ...
> Will we be found guilty in that dreadful day? Or shall we face the righteous Judge with our sins cleansed and our records clear? ...
> Fortunately there is hope. If you apologize for your sins and ask for help, Jesus Himself will help you. He has promised, "I will help you." Isaiah 41:10, RSV. Paul found Christ's offer more than sufficient. He rejoiced, "I can do all things in him who strengthens me." Phil. 4:13, RSV. You don't need to go on in your old sinful way. You can be a new person in Christ, conqueror of every evil tendency, beautiful with a character like the character of the lovely Jesus.

"extrinsic justification" in Galatians by stating that "in justification" his "I" was crucified with Christ. However, contrary to pietistic evangelicalism, Paul's meaning of the crucifixion spoken of in Gal. 2:20 is not a subjective crucifixion but that which took place on the cross of Calvary. See also Froom, *Movement of Destiny,* pp. 207, 267, where justification is said to be by indwelling; Edward Hoehn, "Salvation without the Deeds of the Law," *Review and Herald,* 21 May 1971 (Hoehn says: "What concerned Paul was lack of recognition that no one can make himself righteous in the sight of God. This *transformation* is possible only by the power of Christ living in the heart." [Emphasis supplied.]); Roy Allan Anderson, "Free Indeed," *The Ministry,* Nov. 1976, p. 17, where Anderson says that justification is made possible by Christ's becoming goodness in us.

And then you can face the judgment unafraid. Thank God for Jesus Christ![70]

J. L. Tucker in *It Happened at Night* says:

Describing the characteristics of the saved who are welcomed by Jesus at His second coming, we read, They have the patience of the saints; they keep the commandments of God, and they have the testimony of Jesus Christ. Revelation 14:12. And ... "Blessed are they that do His commandments, that they may have right to the tree of life. ...." Revelation 22:14. The wise thing for each of us to do is to let Jesus come into our hearts and live His beautiful life in us.[71]

The whole context of this statement shows Tucker to mean that salvation is attained by the subjective process of *Christ within*.

If there is a difference between these writers on final acceptance and writers such as Herbert Douglass and C. Mervyn Maxwell, it is that the former fail to take their theological perspective to its ultimate conclusion, whereas the latter follow their views through with strict logical consistency. The former are *implicitly perfectionistic*, while the latter are *explicitly perfectionistic*.

If righteousness by faith is "the goodness of Jesus in us" (R. A. Anderson), *then it is a very short step indeed to the idea that righteousness by faith is perfection.* The final generation, then, are those who perfectly duplicate the sinless character of Jesus. Dr. Douglass writes that Adventists will

... demonstrate to the world that man need not remain a sinner, that man may attain a sinless, righteous experience by the same faith that Jesus exercised, that is, righteousness by faith.
The Adventist invitation to the world is to "come and see". ...[72]

Douglass spells out his equation of righteousness by faith with perfectionism in "The Unique Contribution of Adventist Eschatology."[73] For the associate editor of the *Review and Herald*, the

---

70. Lawrence Maxwell, *Signs of the Times,* June 1975. Lawrence Maxwell is editor of *Signs of the Times.*

71. J. L. Tucker, *It Happened at Night,* pp. 13-14.

72. Herbert E. Douglass, "God Does Not Play Word Games," *The Ministry,* Oct. 1974, p. 37.

73. Herbert E. Douglass, "The Unique Contribution of Adventist Eschatology," esp. pp. 18-33, in Biblical Research Committee, *North American Bible Conference, 1974.*

Conclusion:
The Shaking of Adventism

I

Contemporary Adventism—especially in the 1970's—is in conflict over the nature of the gospel of Paul and the Reformers. Two contrasting elements (Protestant and Roman Catholic) have always been present in the Adventist articulation of the gospel. But in the modern period they have emerged as two full-grown, distinct theologies. The Protestant articulation of the gospel stands on the Christological and soteriological gains of the 1950's and 1960's. The Roman Catholic approach, in order to survive and grow, must sweep aside twenty years of theological development, for it looks upon the Christological and soteriological emphases of the 1950's and 1960's as inimical to its theological existence. If this latter approach triumphs within Seventh-day Adventism, then there is no doubt in this writer's mind that the movement should restate its claim. For how can one *further* the work of the Reformers by taking their gospel and refashioning it according to the gospel of Roman Catholicism?

If Adventism has a distinctive contribution, there is little doubt that it lies in the area of eschatology. Most Reformation scholars would be quick to agree that the Reformation stopped short of a full-blown eschatological perspective consistent with its dogmatic center. However, if the Adventist Church is going to speak seriously of *furthering* the Reformation, she must elucidate her eschatological contribution in a way that *builds* upon rather than *destroys* the foundation laid by the Reformers.

Looking over Adventism's history as a whole, we suspect that the initial claims to furthering the Reformation were made in a fairly general fashion. It is even probable that the Reformation was understood in terms of the theological perspective of the early pioneers. Yet the movement has grown considerably since those times, and it is difficult to see how more informed, sophisticated exponents of the Adventist faith can be as naive in their claim to stand in the Reformation stream. The burden of a more faithful representation of the Reformers rests on the present-day Adventist.

The crux of the problem in modern Adventism lies in understanding *the relation of justification and sanctification*. It was their proper relationship which stood at the heart of the Reformation. No doubt those Adventists who insist that righteousness by faith means justification *and* sanctification do so out of a sincere desire to honor the law of God and avoid the antinomian pitfall. But it is equally true that those who have included sanctification in the article of righteousness by faith have done so against the better judgment of Paul and the Reformers. Further, *inclusion* has resulted in *fusion*.

The height of this approach to righteousness by faith is found in the theology of H. E. Douglass and the *Review and Herald* leadership of the church. Here the gospel is equated with the believer. (Rome and much neo-Protestantism—e.g., Schleiermacher— have done the same thing.) This is the inevitable result of mixing justification and sanctification. In this theology the *medium* (the believer) is the *message*. The infinite *qualitative* distance between the God-man Saviour and those whom He saves is qualified so that there is only a *quantitative* difference. Instead of being the unique Saviour, Jesus becomes the "Model Man." *Imitation* of Christ swallows up faith in His God-man achievement as well as ethical conduct motivated by that achievement. Anyone with the slightest grasp of the Reformation gospel will not fail to see that Douglass' theology is more consistent with Rome than the Reformers. To speak of it as "furthering the work of the Reformation" is to change the meaning of plain words.

I repeat, we must beware of being wiser than Paul and the Reformers in this matter of righteousness by faith. More than once this author has come across the mentality which says, "Sure, that is how righteousness by faith is used in Paul, but we Adventists have chosen to use it *this* way [i.e., to include both justification and sanctification]." This type of approach carries great dangers:

1. The chief danger is that the *distinctive* Adventist use of the expression will drastically alter the Pauline-Reformation use. We believe this has happened.

2. This type of approach encourages the suspicion among evangelicals that Adventists want to stand *over* the Bible instead of *under* the Bible.

3. Even if the different use of a biblical expression did not ultimately alter its meaning, such a use should still be questioned — especially when the expression is one that lies at the heart of the biblical message. This author is reminded of all too many sermons on biblical texts. Although they may not be saying something incorrect, they are not saying what the *text* says. While they may state *theological* truth, the *use* of the text confuses people about what the Bible is saying. People are thus encouraged to move away from the biblical message.

II

In this section I wish to allow myself more liberty than I have in the course of my presentation up to now. The reason is that this project has more than academic interest to me. For one thing, I do not believe that justice is done to the Adventist or his movement if I look at his position from merely a detached academic viewpoint. It is obvious that, in my examination of the central hub of Adventism, the Adventist wishes me to examine myself!

From my own perspective, I cannot help but be deeply interested in the mission of Adventists. I am a churchman who stands in the tradition of the Reformation. Hence, I am more than slightly interested in a movement which unashamedly informs me that it has been raised up by God to carry forward the work of the Reformation in a way that I cannot!

Once I was assured of the fundamental Christian stance of Seventh-day Adventism, I determined to execute my task in the

spirit of one who is open to being taught, even if from an unexpected source. Thus, I intend to be honest and frank, for I believe
that is what a true Adventist would want me to be.

1. To begin with, the Advent movement has, when all things are
considered, done *amazingly well*. From a small, nondescript, and
isolated group of refugees from the Millerite movement, it has
grown into a formidable humanitarian establishment in the world.
Whatever one's creed or candor, he cannot deny this fact.

2. Further, the Adventist is one who is in *utter earnestness* about
the execution of what he believes is his special commission from
God. Irrespective of what one thinks about how well the Adventist
has carried out this commission, the fact that he is a highly zealous
devotee cannot be gainsaid. Nor is this earnestness mere blind
religious enthusiasm in many cases. In the years of my investigation into Adventism, I have encountered a zeal for the doctrine of
justification by faith barely matched anywhere else. Many of the
rank-and-file Adventists I have met are completely "sold" on the
gospel of free justification in Christ.

3. Another aspect of Adventist consciousness deserves commen-
dation. The Adventist is *zealous for the law of God*. Zeal for God's
law and legalism are not synonymous, even though some who are
zealous for the law would encourage us to make the equation.
However, most Adventists that I have encountered are zealous for
God's law as an expression of the reality of justification in the life of
the believer. To state it another way, the Adventist is anxious to
hold justification by grace and judgment according to works in
their proper biblical tension. He believes that so much emphasis on
the former has meant a detraction from the latter. This concern to
hold justification by grace and judgment according to works in
proper tension must be applauded by all who wish to take the
biblical perspective seriously. The proper relating of law and gospel
in one's daily life is important, especially in an age of flabby
sentimentalism and situation ethics.

Having said all this—and in no way intending to detract from
it—I wish to express some perplexing aspects of Adventism which
relate to the central concern of this book:

1. The Adventist community gives considerable evidence of

being *isolationist.*[1] This was particularly the case in the early decades of the movement; and it is still to be found today, though to a lesser degree. The early pioneers of Seventh-day Adventism tended to believe that the Holy Spirit Dove flew straight from the apostles to their own shoulders—with only occasional stopovers in the intervening period. They blithely brushed aside virtually the whole history of doctrinal development in the Christian church.

The price the Adventist community has paid for this is that it has had to repeat the mistakes of the past. It is fascinating to observe how Adventism has re-enacted the doctrinal struggles of the church down the ages. The movement has struggled through a period of dry legalism, the Trinitarian and Christological issues, the question of the nature of the atonement, and now it is embroiled in conflict over soteriology. (It should come as a warning to Adventism that when the Christian church arrived at the soteriological issue in the sixteenth century, there was a serious split in her ranks.) Much needless struggle—and much unnecessary suspicion from other Christians—could have been avoided if the early Adventists could have conceded that the Holy Spirit had been at work well before the "remnant" community arrived on the scene.

This isolationism is still in evidence today. I have come across it more than once in my research into the movement. When, in the spirit of honest inquiry, I visited the General Conference of Seventh-day Adventists at Washington, D.C., I found a reluctance among leaders to be honest about the church's conflict over the nature of the gospel. I met with a real effort to assure me that all was well in the remnant community—when I knew all the while that such was not the case. This publication is a refusal to allow my Adventist brothers the privilege of dealing with the matter in a corner. The reason for my refusal is that I am convinced that the struggle the Adventist Church is undergoing at present is a struggle which concerns all evangelical Christians. And my reason for believing this is what the Adventists themselves have taught me!

Look at it this way: The Adventist has gone to great pains to assure me that God has raised him up to correct my misunderstanding of the Reformation gospel and thereby to stop my slide

---

1. *Isolationist* does not mean being a distinctive denomination but behaving as though no other denomination exists.

toward Roman Catholicism. And yet Adventism is in a life-and-death struggle over the real nature of the gospel within its own ranks. Should I not be interested in that conflict? And should not all "apostate Protestants" be interested in it as well? But who is going to listen to a community about the gospel if that community itself cannot agree on what the gospel is?

I suspect that this is why the leaders of the General Conference attempted to "play down" the struggle when I visited Washington, D.C. They were doubtless afraid that knowledge of this conflict would make their stupendous claim less credible in the Protestant world. However, as I have sought to point out, it is only fair that evangelical Protestants be made aware of the shaking that is taking place within Adventism today.

2. Another feature which I have observed within Adventism is *triumphalism*.[2] Let me be quick to say that if anyone would be tempted to triumphalism, it would be the person who sincerely believes that he is God's latter-day special. However, triumphalism is not intrinsic to the movement, and there are enough warnings in Scripture (e.g., Mark 10:42-45) to keep the Adventist (and for that matter, all of us) on guard. Also, there are enough warnings in Ellen G. White to convince the Adventist that arrogant self-infatuation and the tendency to be a law unto oneself are contrary to the Spirit of prophecy (Rev. 19:10).

A triumphalistic church and a triumphalistic leadership will not be quick to repent and to openly acknowledge mistakes. Unqualified admission that mistakes have been made are rare in Adventism.

------

2. Consider the following as an example of *triumphalism*. At a General Conference worship, Jan. 9, 1976, Robert H. Pierson said: "When you and I joined the General Conference family something special happened to us. When we begin work in the General Conference office we become part of what inspiration describes as *God's highest authority on earth*. ... All of us are something special in God's sight. Our relationship to our church, to the world field, to one another, and to the work entrusted to us is unique. We are part of 'the highest authority that God has on earth.'... These three buildings are not ordinary buildings. ... These buildings constitute a consecrated place where God, through His appointed servants — *you, me* — directs His worldwide work. ... As those of us here on the General Conference staff continue our unique service for Him, let us remember that we are daily, hourly, momentarily a part of a group of leaders that constitute the highest authority of God upon earth ..." (Robert H. Pierson, *The Ministry,* June 1976). Pope Paul, please take note! (A thoughtful observer could not but see that this Rome-like ecclesiology springs from a soteriology of the same character.)

Take for example the period of the 1950's to the 1970's. The book, *Questions on Doctrine,* was a real break with past Adventist teaching on Christology, especially the matter of the sinful human nature of Christ. Yet to my knowledge there was not one open acknowledgment of this to either the rank-and-file members of the Adventist Church or to the evangelical Protestant world. Why? Why was it covered up by saying that only a few on the "lunatic fringe" held and taught what had actually been the Adventist position before that time?

At present there is evidence of a retraction of what was written in *Questions on Doctrine.* I have heard Adventist leaders speak of it as "damnable heresy." I have seen letters from Washington, D.C., making it plain that the present leadership of the church is much opposed to the book. Once again, there is not one open statement to this effect. Quite apart from evangelical Protestants who were led to believe that *Questions on Doctrine* represents the official mind of the church, many rank-and-file Adventists are in confusion about its present status among church leaders. Why all the silence? Does the Adventist leadership not wish the evangelical Protestant world to know that it has made some big mistakes?

Take also the matter of the leadership's conflict with Robert Brinsmead in the 1960's. It opposed Brinsmead and made use of Dr. Heppenstall and Dr. Ford in the process. Then, in the 1970's Brinsmead was converted to Heppenstall and Ford's position. One would expect the leaders to be overjoyed. Yet the well-nigh inexplicable fact is that the church leaders—via the *Review and Herald* in particular—have embraced Brinsmead's old position and, in the case of Dr. Ford at least, have brought their previous powerful instruments under pressure. The point I wish to make is this: *Not one word of public acknowledgment concerning this about-face has come from the leadership of the church.* There is only astounding silence about the fact that what was opposed in the 1960's is now embraced. Why the lack of candor? Is this leadership *able* to truly repent?

In reviewing the central thrust of Adventism, I have been intrigued to observe the striking parallels between the leadership's behavior at the time of the 1888 revival and the role of the leadership today in the current conflict. Is the present shaking 1888 *redivivus?* Let me cite a few examples of what I speak about.

In discussing issues with some of the church's leaders in Washington, D.C., I met with the assurance that there "isn't an Advent-ist in the land who doesn't know what justification by faith alone is." Did not Uriah Smith, then editor of the *Review and Herald,* say exactly the same thing in response to the revival that Waggoner and Jones were bringing?[3]

Likewise, the great fear of Uriah Smith was that the *new* emphasis of Waggoner and Jones was similar to the doctrine of Protestant "Babylonians." Has not this same response been forthcoming in the present shaking? Have there not been fears expressed that the new emphasis on justification within Adventism is an adoption of "Babylonian" Protestant religion?

Furthermore, both in the 1888 crisis and in the present struggle, I have observed the call back to "historic" Adventism by those in opposition to the revival of justification by faith.

How can the Seventh-day Adventist Church call the evangelical Protestant churches to repentance when she gives little evidence — particularly among her leadership — of knowing what real repentance actually is? Perhaps, in light of some references to repentance in recent issues of the *Review and Herald,* I should make clear that I am referring to repentance on central theological matters and not to window-dressing repentance on side issues. Of course, what I say to my brethren in the Adventist community I say to my own denomination and to Christians everywhere. Let us pray that we shall not be like Esau, who sought repentance and did not find it.

3. There is the Adventist *fear of antinomianism.* No one who wishes to take the Bible seriously should quibble at this fear. We mention it here not to criticize it as such, but rather to draw attention to the unhealthy office that it frequently holds in Adventism.

The fear of antinomianism often drives the Adventist into the opposite error of legalism. Both legalism and antinomianism are to be avoided. Both errors seek to rob God of His glory. But the Adventist must beware of thinking that legalism is the lesser of the two evils.

---

3. Uriah Smith, "Our Righteousness," *Review and Herald,* 11 June 1889; idem, "Our Righteousness Again," ibid., 2 July 1889.

The attempt within Adventism to place sanctification in the article of righteousness by faith is an effort to avoid antinomianism. There is the fear that, if justification is stressed, sanctification will be given lesser stress. But this fear is not biblical. Not only is it not biblical, but excluding sanctification from the article of righteousness by faith actually ends antinomianism. The law is only honored when there is an unqualified acknowledgment that all of its demands, in their severest dimension, are met in the doing and dying of Jesus, the God-man. This is the good news! However, when it is suggested that the believer's keeping of the law constitutes a part of the good news (or the whole!), as in the theology of Douglass, then the law is dishonored. For *all the efforts of the believer in this life never reach the standard of God Himself in the God-man, Jesus of Nazareth.* The Adventist community must overcome the type of reaction to antinomianism that results in legalism if it is to show the Protestant world the proper relation between the law and the gospel.

4. Finally, I wish to comment on *the use of Ellen G. White* in the present shaking within Adventism. When I interpret Mrs. White at her best, I hear her calling the Adventist community back to the Bible as the final norm in all matters of controversy: "The Bible is to be presented as the word of the infinite God, as the end of all controversy and the foundation of all faith."[4] Yet in the present shaking within Adventism, I have observed a frantic rushing to the voluminous writings of Ellen White to find statements that will score a point against the opponent. This is to say nothing of the dreaded "compilations" which wrench this saying and that saying out of context and then place them side by side to form the authoritative last word in the struggle. This type of action neither honors the Bible nor Mrs. White. It is a sad sign of a people who take another human being—however gifted and used of God—and place her above the Bible and herself.

That is not all. I mentioned that Mrs. White wrote voluminously. Those writings took place over a considerable period of time. They took place in specific contexts, and they stood in a definite relationship to each other. To use those writings correctly (so as not to

4. Ellen G. White, *Christ's Object Lessons,* pp. 39-40.

misrepresent them) requires a great deal more skill than is generally being exhibited. I know for a fact that some scholars within Adventism are very concerned over the superficial and childish use made of Ellen White's writings. She has a wax nose. She is turned this way, and then that way, and then this way again. If Adventists wish to bring Mrs. White to the place where she has no authority at all in their movement, let them keep using her writings as a source for point-scoring in their intra-church squabbles. The final end of being made to take all positions is to take no position at all!

I fear very deeply that the use made of Mrs. White in Seventh-day Adventism is testimony to an un-Protestant attitude toward the Bible. I fear that many Adventists have a Roman Catholic (can we even say that any more?) belief that the Bible is too difficult for rank-and-file Christians to understand. In place of the Bible, they turn to Mrs. White to tell them what God says. The leaders, theologians, and pastors of the church must accept the blame for this state of affairs. Who else has taught the laity to behave this way? Let me say clearly that, so long as this situation exists, Adventism has no hope of influencing evangelical Protestants who claim the Reformers—with their *sola Scriptura* (the Bible alone)—as their forefathers.

I conclude with a charge to the church's leaders, theologians, and pastors:

> The Bible, and the Bible alone, is to be our creed, the sole bond of union; all who bow to this Holy Word will be in harmony. Our own views and ideas must not control our efforts. Man is fallible, but God's Word is infallible. Instead of wrangling with one another, let men exalt the Lord. Let us meet all opposition as did our Master, saying, "It is written." Let us lift up the banner on which is inscribed, The Bible our rule of faith and discipline.[5]

---

5. E. G. White, *Selected Messages,* 1:416.

Bibliography

Aflame for God. Washington, D.C.: Review & Herald Pub. Assn., 1951. Addresses and panel discussion of the 1950 pre-General Conference Session council of the Seventh-day Adventist Ministerial Association.

Althaus, Paul. *The Theology of Martin Luther*. Translated by R. C. Schultz. Philadelphia: Fortress Press, 1970.

Andreasen, M. L. *The Book of Hebrews*. Washington, D.C.: Review & Herald Pub. Assn., 1948.

———. *Letters to the Churches*. Conway, Mo.: Gems of Truth, n.d. [c. 1958].

———. *The Sanctuary Service*. 2nd ed., rev. Washington, D.C.: Review & Herald Pub. Assn., 1947.

Andrews, John Nevins. *Sermons on the Two Covenants*. Battle Creek, Mich.: Seventh-day Adventist Pub. Assn., 1875.

———. *Thoughts on the Sabbath and the Perpetuity of the Law of God*. Paris, Maine: James White, 1851.

Awake and Sing! N.p., n.d. [c. 1969]. Songbook compiled by supporters of Robert D. Brinsmead.

Barth, Karl. *Church Dogmatics*. Edited by G. W. Bromiley and T. F. Torrance. Translated by G. W. Bromiley. Edinburgh: T. & T. Clark, 1956.

———. *The Epistle to the Romans*. 6th ed. Translated by Edwyn C. Hoskyns, 1933. New York: Oxford University Press, 1976.

Basham, F. A. "A Paper Presented to the Biblical Research Committee of the Australasian Division on the Subject of 'Righteousness by Faith,' 3 Feb. 1976."

Berkhof, Louis. *Systematic Theology*. London: Banner of Truth Trust, 1963.

Berkouwer, G. C. *Faith and Justification*. Grand Rapids: Wm. B. Eerdmans Pub. Co., 1963.

Biblical Research Committee of the General Conference, ed., *North American Bible Conference, 1974*. Washington, D.C.: General Conference of Seventh-day Adventists, 1974. Papers presented at the 1974 North American Division Bible conferences.

Bird, Herbert S. *Theology of Seventh-day Adventism*. Grand Rapids: Wm. B. Eerdmans Pub. Co., 1961.

Bouyer, Louis. *The Spirit and Forms of Protestantism*. Translated by A.
V. Littledale. Westminster, Md.: Newman Press, 1956.

Branson, W. H. *Drama of the Ages*. Nashville: Southern Pub. Assn.,
1950.

———. *How Men Are Saved*. Nashville: Southern Pub. Assn., 1941.

———. *The Way to Christ*. Washington, D.C.: Review & Herald Pub.
Assn., n.d. [c. 1948].

Brinsmead, Robert D. "All Things Are Ready." Edited by Dawn Mul-
roney, Perth, W. A., Australia. A mimeographed report of a sermon
presented Dec., 1976.

———. *An Answer to "Conflicting Concepts of Righteousness by Faith
in the Seventh-day Adventist Church."* Edited by David McMahon.
Sydney: Wittenberg Steam Press Pub. Assn., 1976.

———. *The Current Righteousness by Faith Dialogue*. N.p., 1975. A
"Thought Paper."

———. *A Doctrinal Analysis of "The History and Teaching of Robert
Brinsmead."* Los Angeles: Sanctuary Awakening Fellowship, n.d.
[c. 1962].

———. *The Open Door*. N.p., 1959.

———. *A Review of the Awakening Message*. 2 pts. N.p., 1972-73.

———. *Sanctuary Institute Syllabus IV: Original Sin*. Snohomish,
Wash.: Prophetic Research International, 1968.

———. *A Statement to My S.D.A. Friends*. N.p., n.d. [1974].

———. *Tidings of Great Joy*. Baker, Oreg.: Hudson Printing Co., 1960.

———. *The Timing of Revelation 18 and the Perfecting of the Saints: An
Answer to Dr. Desmond Ford and Pastor L. C. Naden*. N.p., 1969.

———. *Weighed in the Balances*. Baker, Oreg.: Hudson Printing Co.,
1960.

Buchanan, James. *The Doctrine of Justification*. 1867. Reprint. London:
Banner of Truth Trust, 1961.

Bush, Francis F. *How a Pastor Meets the Brinsmead Issue*. South Lan-
caster, Mass., 1968.

Butler, George I. *The Law in the Book of Galatians: Is It the Moral Law,
or Does It Refer to that System of Law Peculiarly Jewish?* Battle
Creek, Mich.: Seventh-day Adventist Pub. Assn., 1886.

Calvin, John. *Calvin: Theological Treatises*. Translated by J.K.S. Reid.
Library of Christian Classics, vol. 22. London: S.C.M. Press, 1954.

———. *Institutes of the Christian Religion*. Edited by John T. McNeill.
Translated by Ford Lewis Battles. Library of Christian Classics,
vols. 20-21. London: S.C.M. Press, 1961.

———. *Institutes of the Christian Religion*. Translated by Henry Beveridge. 2 vols. Grand Rapids: Wm. B. Eerdmans Pub. Co., 1970.

Chemnitz, Martin. *Examination of the Council of Trent*. Pt. 1. Translated by Fred Kramer. St. Louis: Concordia Pub. House, 1971.

Christian, Lewis Harrison. *The Fruitage of Spiritual Gifts: The Influence and Guidance of Ellen G. White in the Advent Movement*. Washington, D.C.: Review & Herald Pub. Assn., 1947.

Clifford, A. John and Russell R. Standish. *Conflicting Concepts of Righteousness by Faith in the Seventh-day Adventist Church: Australasian Division*. Victoria, Australia: published by the authors, 1976. Biblical Research Institute paper.

Cottrell, Raymond F. *Perfection in Christ*. Washington, D.C.: Review & Herald Pub. Assn., 1965.

Cottrell, Roswell F. *The Bible Class: Lessons upon the Law of God, and the Faith of Jesus*. Rochester, N.Y.: Advent Review Office, 1855.

Daniells, Arthur G. *Christ Our Righteousness*. Washington, D.C.: Review & Herald Pub. Assn., 1941.

Daujat, Jean. *The Theology of Grace*. Translated by a nun of Stanbrook Abbey. New York: Hawthorne Books, 1959.

Defense Literature Committee of the General Conference of Seventh-day Adventists. *The History and Teaching of Robert Brinsmead*. Washington, D.C.: Review & Herald Pub. Assn., 1968.

————. *Perfection*. Washington, D.C.: Defense Literature Committee, 1965.

————. *Some Current Errors in Brinsmead Teachings*. Washington, D.C.: Defense Literature Committee, 1963.

De Senarclens, Jacques. *Heirs of the Reformation*. Edited and translated by G. W. Bromiley. London, S.C.M. Press, 1963.

Douglass, Herbert E. *Jesus, the Model Man*. Adult Sabbath School Lesson Quarterly, April-June 1977. Warburton, Vict., Australia: Signs Pub. Co., 1977.

———— and Leo R. Van Dolson. *Jesus, the Benchmark of Humanity*. Nashville: Southern Pub. Assn., 1976.

————, Edward Heppenstall, Hans K. LaRondelle, and C. Mervyn Maxwell. *Perfection: The Impossible Possibility*. Nashville: Southern Pub. Assn., 1975.

Douty, Norman F. *Another Look at Seventh-day Adventism*. Grand Rapids: Baker Book House, 1962.

Errors of the Brinsmead Teachings. Conway, Mo.: Gems of Truth, 1961. Includes a copy of a special committee report of the General Conference of Seventh-day Adventists.

Evans, I. H. *This Is the Way*. Washington, D.C.: Review & Herald Pub. Assn. 1939.

Everson, Charles T. "Saved by Grace." In *Typical Evangelistic Sermons*.

Washington, D.C.: Review & Herald Pub. Assn., 1940. A sermon reprint.

Executive Committee of the Australasian Division of Seventh-day Adventists. *Righteousness by Faith*. Warburton, Vict., Australia: Signs Pub. Co., 1959.

Ford, Desmond. "An Answer to Dr. Russell Standish." A mimeographed transcript of a sermon presented Oct. 2, 1976, at Avondale College, Cooranbong, N.S.W., Australia.

———. *Redemption, Objective and Subjective*. N.p., n.d.

———. *Unlocking God's Treasury*. Warburton, Vict., Australia: Signs Pub. Co., 1964.

Ford, Gillian (Mrs. Desmond). *The Soteriological Implications of the Human Nature of Christ*. Cooranbong, N.S.W., Australia: Avondale College, n.d. [1975].

Freeman, Paul H., ed. *Evaluation of Brinsmead Doctrine*. Santa Ana, Calif.: Paul H. Freeman, 1968. Refutation by Edward Heppenstall; defense by Jack Zwemer.

Froom, LeRoy Edwin. *The Coming of the Comforter*. Rev. ed. Washington, D.C.: Review & Herald Pub. Assn., 1947.

———. *The Conditionalist Faith of Our Fathers*. 2 vols. Washington, D.C.: Review & Herald Pub. Assn., 1966.

———. *Eternal Verities Triumphant*. A syllabus prepared for union and local ministerial retreats and workers' meetings, 1963-66.

———. *Movement of Destiny*. Washington, D.C.: Review & Herald Pub. Assn., 1971.

———. *Prophetic Faith of Our Fathers*. 4 vols. Washington, D.C.: Review & Herald Pub. Assn., 1950.

Gane, Erwin R. "Christ and Human Perfection." Essay published together with Edward Heppenstall, "Some Theological Considerations of Perfection," and Robert W. Olson, "Outline Studies on Christian Perfection and Original Sin," in supplement to *The Ministry*. Washington, D.C.: General Conference Ministerial Assn., n.d.

———. "Is There Power in Justification?" Paper produced at Pacific Union College, Angwin, Calif. N.d. [c. 1977].

Griffith Thomas, W. H. *The Principles of Theology*. London: Church Book Room Press, 1963.

"M. H." *The Two Laws, and Two Covenants*. Battle Creek, Mich., n.d. [c. 1858].

Haddock, Robert. "A History of the Doctrine of the Sanctuary in the Advent Movement: 1800-1905." B.D. thesis, Andrews University, 1970.

Hatton, Max. *Jesus Our Example*. Goodlettsville, Tenn.: Jack D. Walker,

1977. A brief examination of the Adult Sabbath School Lesson Quarterly for April-June, 1977, *Jesus, the Model Man*, by Herbert E. Douglass.

Hawley, Don. *Getting It All Together*. Washington, D.C.: Review & Herald Pub. Assn., 1974.

Haynes, Carlyle B. *The Hour of God's Judgment*. Mountain View, Calif.: Pacific Press Pub. Assn., 1926.

———. *Righteousness in Christ*. Washington, D.C.: Seventh-day Adventist Ministerial Assn., n.d.

Heppenstall, Edward. "Some Theological Considerations of Perfection." Essay published together with Erwin R. Gane, "Christ and Human Perfection," and Robert W. Olson, "Outline Studies on Christian Perfection and Original Sin," in supplement to *The Ministry*. Washington, D. C.: General Conference Ministerial Assn., n.d.

Hoekema, Anthony A. *The Four Major Cults*. Grand Rapids: Wm. B. Eerdmans Pub. Co., 1963.

Hudson, A. L., ed. *A Warning and Its Reception*. Baker, Oreg.: Hudson Printing Co., n.d. [c. 1960].

———, ed. *Witnessing a Metamorphosis*. Baker, Oreg.: Hudson Printing Co., n.d. [c. 1959]. A compilation of articles by Donald Grey Barnhouse and Walter Martin appearing in *Eternity* magazine and articles by E. Schuyler English and Walter Martin appearing in *Our Hope* magazine. There is also the record of a conversation between Barnhouse and A. L. Hudson "relative to the relationship between the editors of *Eternity* magazine and the General Conference of Seventh-day Adventists."

Jacobs, Henry Eyster and John A. W. Haas, eds. *The Lutheran Cyclopedia*. New York: Charles Scribner's Sons, 1911.

Jones, Alonzo T. *The Revelation of God*. Battle Creek, Mich.: Good Health Pub. Co., n.d. [c. 1904].

Karolyi, A. M. *Errors of the Brinsmead Teachings*. Rev. ed. Syracuse, N. Y.: New York Conference of Seventh-day Adventists, n.d. [c. mid-1960's].

Kittel, Gerhard and Gerhard Friedrich. *Theological Dictionary of the New Testament*. Translated by G. W. Bromiley. 9 vols. Grand Rapids: Wm. B. Eerdmans Pub. Co., 1964-74.

Kluzit, Victor P. *An Appeal to Withdraw and Make a Public Confession for the Sabbath School Quarterly Entitled "Jesus, the Model Man" April-June, 1977 (Lev. 26:40, 42)*. Goodlettsville, Tenn.: Jack D. Walker, 1977.

Kung, Hans. *Justification: The Doctrine of Karl Barth and a Catholic Reflection*. London: Burns & Oates, 1964.

LaRondelle, Hans K. "Fitness for Heaven: A Dialogue with Robert Brinsmead on Bible Perfection." N.d. [c. 1967].

————. "Kommentar van dr. h. k. la rondelle op het artikel van paxton in jeugd, november, 1976" [Commentary of Dr. H. K. LaRondelle on the Article of Paxton in *Youth*, November, 1976].

————. *Perfection and Perfectionism: A Dogmatic-Ethical Study of Biblical Perfection and Phenomenal Perfectionism*. J. H. Kok, N. V. Kempen, 1971. Andrews University Monographs, Studies in Religion, vol. 3. Berrien Springs, Mich.: Andrews University Press, 1975.

————. "Righteousness by Faith." Seminary lectures presented in 1966 at Andrews University, Berrien Springs, Mich.

————. "Seventh-day Adventist Statement on Righteousness by Faith." 1975.

Lehman, J. W. "What Is Righteousness?" Loma Linda, Calif.: Sermons for Pastors, n.d. [1975]. A series of four cassette tapes.

Leith, John H., ed. *Creeds of the Churches*. Rev. ed. Garden City, N. Y.: Doubleday & Co., Anchor Books, 1973.

Lowe, Harry W. *Redeeming Grace*. Mountain View, Calif.: Pacific Press Pub. Assn., 1968.

Luther, Martin. *The Bondage of the Will*. Edited and translated by J. I. Packer and O. R. Johnston. London: James Clarke & Co., 1957.

————. *D. Martin Luthers Werke: Kritische Gesammtausgabe*. Weimar: H. Bohlau, 1883-.

————. *Luther and Erasmus: Free Will and Salvation*. Library of Christian Classics, vol. 17. Philadelphia: Westminster Press, 1969.

————. *Luther's Works*. American edition. General editors, Jaroslav Pelikan and Helmut T. Lehmann. 55 vols. St. Louis: Concordia Pub. House; Philadelphia: Fortress Press, 1955-75.

MacGuire, Meade. *The Life of Victory*. Washington, D. C.: Review & Herald Pub. Assn., 1924.

Martin, Walter. *The Truth About Seventh-day Adventism*. London: Marshall, Morgan & Scott, 1960.

Maxwell, Arthur S. *Protestantism Imperilled*. Warburton, Vict., Australia: Signs Pub. Co., n.d. [1940's].

McFarland, J. W. and J. R. Spangler. *Century 21: Institute for Better Living*. Washington, D. C.: Review & Herald Pub. Assn., 1977.

McMahon, David. *E. J. Waggoner: The Myth and the Man*. Sydney: Wittenberg Steam Press Pub. Assn., forthcoming.

Melanchthon, Philipp. *Loci Communes Theologici*. Library of Christian Classics, vol. 19. Philadelphia: Westminster Press, 1969.

Mozley, J. F. *William Tyndale*. New York: Macmillan Co., n.d. [1937].

Mueller, John. *Christian Dogmatics*. St. Louis: Concordia Pub. House, 1934.

Naden, L. C. *In Quest of Holiness*. Warburton, Vict., Australia: Signs Pub. Co., 1968.

————. *The Perfecting of the Saints*. Warburton, Vict., Australia: Signs Pub. Co., 1968.

————. *What Do the Brinsmead Faction Really Believe?* Published by the author, n.d. [c. 1960].

Neis, Richard. "Jesus, the Model Man." Loma Linda, Calif.: Study Tapes, 11443 Richmont Rd., 1977. A cassette tape.

Nichol, Francis D. *Answers to Objections*. Washington, D.C.: Review & Herald Pub. Assn., 1952.

Olson, A. V *Through Crisis to Victory: 1888-1901*. Washington, D.C.: Review & Herald Pub. Assn., 1966.

Olson, Robert W. "Outline Studies on Christian Perfection and Original Sin." Essay published together with Erwin R. Gane, "Christ and Human Perfection," and Edward Heppenstall, "Some Theological Considerations of Perfection," in supplement to *The Ministry*. Washington, D.C.: General Conference Ministerial Assn., n.d.

Onjukka, Lauri. *The Sanctuary and Perfection*. N.p., 1970.

Orr, James. *The Progress of Dogma*. New York: A. C. Armstrong & Son, 1901.

Our Firm Foundation. 2 vols. Washington, D.C.: Review & Herald Pub. Assn., 1952. A report of the Seventh-day Adventist Bible conference held Sept. 1-13, 1952, in the Sligo Seventh-day Adventist Church, Takoma Park, Md.

Pease, Norval F. *By Faith Alone*. Mountain View, Calif.: Pacific Press Pub. Assn., 1962.

————. "Justification and Righteousness by Faith in the Seventh-day Adventist Church before 1900." Masters thesis, Seventh-day Adventist Theological Seminary, 1945.

Peiper, Francis. *Christian Dogmatics*. 3 vols. St. Louis: Concordia Pub. House, 1950.

Pierson, Robert H. *We Still Believe*. Washington, D.C.: Review & Herald Pub. Assn., 1975.

Plass, Ewald M., comp. *What Luther Says*. 3 vols. St. Louis: Concordia Pub. House, 1959.

Prescott, W. W. *The Saviour of the World*. Washington, D.C.: Review & Herald Pub. Assn., n.d. [c. 1929].

Price, George McCready. *The Greatest of the Prophets*. Mountain View, Calif.: Pacific Press Pub. Assn., 1955.

Quick Look at Seventh-day Adventists. N.p., 1976. A flyer distributed by Seventh-day Adventists.

Robinson, William Childs. *The Reformation: A Rediscovery of Grace*. Grand Rapids: Wm. B. Eerdmans Pub. Co., 1962.

St. John, H. A. *The Sun of Righteousness*. Bible Student's Library, no. 97. Oakland: Pacific Press Pub. Co., 1892.

Sargeant, E. N. *Brinsmead*. N.p., n.d. [c. 1965].

Seventh-day Adventist Bible Commentary. Edited by Francis D. Nichol. Commentary Reference Series, vols. 1-7. Washington, D.C.: Review & Herald Pub. Assn., 1952-57.

Seventh-day Adventist Encyclopedia. Edited by Don F. Neufeld. Commentary Reference Series, vol. 10. Rev. ed. Washington, D.C.: Review & Herald Pub. Assn., 1976.

Seventh-day Adventists Answer Questions on Doctrine. Washington, D.C.: Review & Herald Pub. Assn., 1957. "Prepared by a Representative Group of Seventh-day Adventist Leaders, Bible Teachers, and Editors."

Short, Donald K. and Robert J. Wieland. *1888 Re-examined*. Strafford, Mo.: Gems of Truth, n.d. [c. 1966].

Slade, Edwin Keck. *The Way of Life*. Washington, D.C.: Review & Herald Pub. Assn., 1929.

Slade, John A. *Lessons from a Detour: A Survey of My Experience in the Brinsmead Movement*. N.p., 1964.

Smith, Uriah. *A Declaration of the Fundamental Principles of the Seventh-day Adventists*. Battle Creek: Seventh-day Adventist Pub. Assn., 1872.

————. *The Sanctuary and the Twenty-three Hundred Days of Daniel VIII. 14*. Battle Creek: Seventh-day Adventist Pub. Assn., 1877.

Spalding, Arthur W. *Captains of the Host*. Washington, D.C.: Review & Herald Pub. Assn., 1949.

————. *Origin and History of Seventh-day Adventists*. 4 vols. Washington, D.C.: Review & Herald Pub. Assn., 1961-62. A revision of *Captains of the Host*.

Spitz, Lewis W., ed. *The Protestant Reformation*. Englewood Cliffs, N.J.: Prentice-Hall, 1966.

Starkey, Alan. *Basic Brinsmead Belief*. Washington, D.C.: Defense Literature Committee of the General Conference of Seventh-day Adventists, 1967.

Steinweg, Bruno William. "Developments in the Teaching of Justification and Righteousness by Faith in the Seventh-day Adventist Church after 1900." Masters thesis, Seventh-day Adventist Theological Seminary, 1948.

Stephens, P. Gregory. *The Life of Grace*. Foundations of Catholic Theology Series. Englewood Cliffs, N.J.: Prentice-Hall, 1963.

Strong, Augustus H. *Systematic Theology*. 3 vols. 1907. Reprint (3 vols. in 1). Valley Forge, Penn.: Judson Press, 1976.

Tappert, Theodore G., ed. and trans. *The Book of Concord*. Philadelphia: Fortress Press, 1959.

Torrance, T. F. and J. K. S. Reed, eds. "Eschatology." *"Scottish Journal of Theology" Occasional Papers*, no. 2. London: Oliver & Boyd, 1957.

Tucker, J. L. *It Happened At Night*. Redlands, Calif.: Quiet Hour, n.d. A Quiet Hour radio program Book of the Month.

Vick, E. W. *Let Me Assure You*. Mountain View, Calif.: Pacific Press Pub. Assn., n.d.

Waggoner, E. J. *Bible Studies on the Book of Romans*. Baker, Oreg.: A. L. Hudson, n.d. A facsimile reproduction from the 1891 General Conference Bulletin.

———. *Christ and His Righteousness*. Oakland: Pacific Press Pub. Co., 1890.

———. *Confession of Faith*. N.p., n.d. [1916]. A letter published posthumously by friends of E. J. Waggoner.

———. *The Everlasting Gospel*. Oakland: Pacific Press Pub. Co., 1900.

———. *The Glad Tidings*. Oakland: Pacific Press Pub. Co., 1900.

———. *The Gospel in Creation*. Oakland: Pacific Press Pub. Co., 1894.

———. *The Gospel in Galatians*. Oakland: Pacific Press Pub. Co., n.d. [c. Dec. 1888]. Comprised of a letter to George I. Butler dated Feb. 10, 1887.

———. *The Power of Forgiveness*. London: International Tract Society, n.d. [c. late 1890's].

Waggoner, J. H. *Justification by Faith*. Oakland: Pacific Press Pub. Co., 1889.

Walker, Jack D., ed. *Documents from the Palmdale Conference on Righteousness by Faith*. Goodlettsville, Tenn.: Jack D. Walker, 1976.

Wallace, R. S. *Calvin's Doctrine of the Christian Life*. Grand Rapids: Wm. B. Eerdmans Pub. Co., 1961.

Warfield, Benjamin B. *Perfectionism*. Edited by Samuel G. Craig. Philadelphia: Presbyterian & Reformed Pub. Co., 1958.

White, Ellen G. *The Acts of the Apostles*. Mountain View, Calif.: Pacific Press Pub. Assn., 1911.

———. *The Adventist Home*. Nashville: Southern Pub. Assn., 1952.

———. *Child Guidance*. Nashville: Southern Pub. Assn., 1954.

———. *Christ's Object Lessons*. Mountain View, Calif.: Pacific Press Pub. Assn., 1900.

———. *The Desire of Ages*. Mountain View, Calif.: Pacific Press Pub. Assn., 1898.

———. *Gospel Workers*. Washington, D.C.: Review & Herald Pub. Assn., 1892.

_____. *The Great Controversy*. Mountain View, Calif.: Pacific Press Pub. Assn., 1911.

_____. *In Heavenly Places*. Washington, D.C.: Review & Herald Pub. Assn., 1967.

_____. *The Ministry of Healing*. Mountain View, Calif.: Pacific Press Pub. Assn., 1905.

_____. *My Life Today*. Washington, D.C.: Review & Herald Pub. Assn., 1952.

_____. *Prophets and Kings*. Mountain View, Calif.: Pacific Press Pub. Assn., 1917.

_____. *The Sanctified Life*. Washington, D.C.: Review & Herald Pub. Assn., 1937.

_____. *Selected Messages*. 2 vols. Washington, D.C.: Review & Herald Pub. Assn., 1958.

_____. *Steps to Christ*. Washington, D.C.: Review & Herald Pub. Assn., 1908.

_____. *Testimonies for the Church*. 9 vols. Mountain View, Calif.: Pacific Press Pub. Assn., 1885-1909.

_____. *Testimonies to Ministers and Gospel Workers*. Mountain View, Calif.: Pacific Press Pub. Assn., 1923.

White, James. *Bible Adventism; or Sermons on the Coming and Kingdom of Our Lord Jesus Christ*. Facsimile ed. Nashville: Southern Pub. Assn., 1972.

_____. *Life Incidents in Connection with the Great Advent Movement*. Battle Creek: Seventh-day Adventist Pub. Assn., 1868.

_____. *Life Sketches of James White and Ellen G. White*. Battle Creek: Seventh-day Adventist Pub. Assn., 1880.

_____. *The Redeemer and Redeemed; or, the Plan of Redemption through Christ*. Oakland: Pacific Seventh-day Adventist Pub. Assn., 1877.

Wilcox, M. C. *Justification, Regeneration, Sanctification*. Oakland: Pacific Press Pub. Co., 1891.

_____. *The More Abundant Life*. Washington, D.C.: Review & Herald Pub. Assn., 1939.

_____. *Studies in Romans*. Mountain View, Calif.: Pacific Press Pub. Assn., 1930.

Periodicals

Australasian Record. Official publication of the Seventh-day Adventist Church, Australasian Division. Signs Pub. Co., Warburton, Vict., Australia.

Christianity Today. A Fortnightly Magazine of Evangelical Conviction. P. O. Box 3800, Greenwich, Conn. 06830.

Eternity. Evangelical Ministries, Inc., 1716 Spruce St., Philadelphia, Penn. 19103.

Ministry, The. Official organ of the Ministerial Association of Seventh-day Adventists. Review & Herald Pub. Assn., 6856 Eastern Ave., N. W., Washington, D. C. 20012.

Present Truth. A publication of New Reformation Fellowship, P.O. Box 1311, Fallbrook, Calif. 92028.

Present Truth, The. A Seventh-day Adventist semi-monthly published 1917-55. Review & Herald Pub. Assn., Washington, D. C. (1917-47); Pacific Press Pub. Assn., Mountain View, Calif. (1948-55).

Protestant Magazine, The. A Seventh-day Adventist publication edited by W. W. Prescott for its duration (1909-15). Review & Herald Pub. Assn., Washington, D. C.

Review and Herald. General church paper of Seventh-day Adventists. Review & Herald Pub. Assn., 6856 Eastern Ave., N. W., Washington, D. C. 20012.

Signs of the Times. A Seventh-day Adventist monthly. Pacific Press Pub. Assn., Mountain View, Calif.

Signs of the Times. Australian ed. A Seventh-day Adventist monthly. Signs Pub. Co., Warburton, Vict., Australia.

Index of Seventh-day Adventist Persons

This index is a listing of representative Seventh-day Adventist authors cited in this book.

Anderson, Roy Allen—83, 86, 87, 88, 88n, 141n, 142

Andreasen, M. L.—72, 76, 76n, 83, 88, 88n, 95, 97n, 109, 109n, 113, 126, 128

Andrews, John Nevins—58n

Basham, F. A.—128, 129, 129n, 130

Bollman, Calvin P.—71

Brainard, F. E.—119, 119n

Branson, W. H.—71, 71n, 72, 72n, 73, 73n, 75n, 92, 93n, 94, 94n, 95, 95n, 96, 97n, 98, 103, 109, 113, 126

Bunch, Taylor—112n, 113n

Bush, Francis F.—107n

Butler, George I.—58, 59n, 73, 73n, 92

Christian, Lewis Harrison—31

Clifford, F. G.—119, 119n

Clifford, A. John—128n, 139, 139n, 144, 144n, 145

Collier, Gordon—97n

Cottrell, Raymond F.—112n

Cottrell, Roswell F.—57, 58n

Daniells, Arthur G.—30, 30n, 31, 32, 70, 70n, 75, 75n, 140

Dick, Ernest D.—85, 86, 91

Douglass, Herbert E.—124, 126, 126n, 128, 133, 133n, 135n, 142, 142n, 143, 143n, 144, 148, 155

Escobar, Arthur S.—89n

Evans, I. H.—76n

Everson, Charles T.—70, 70n

Ford, Desmond—33, 102n, 103n, 104, 106, 110, 112n, 113n, 115, 116, 116n, 117, 117n, 119, 121, 122, 124, 127, 128, 130, 130n, 131, 131n, 132, 133, 135, 136, 136n, 137, 137n, 139, 139n, 144, 153

Ford, Gillian (Mrs. Desmond)—128, 129, 139n, 145n

Froom, LeRoy Edwin—21, 21n, 22, 22n, 24, 27, 27n, 28n, 29n, 32, 34, 57n, 60, 60n, 64, 65, 65n, 66n, 68, 70, 70n, 83, 87, 88, 88n, 89, 90, 90n, 91, 91n, 93, 94n, 95n, 97n

Gane, Erwin R.—111n, 140, 140n

Haddock, Robert—68, 68n

Hatton, Max—134, 134n

Hawley, Don—138, 138n

Haynes, Carlyle B.—20, 20n, 75n

Heppenstall, Edward—93, 93n, 95, 96, 102n, 104, 105, 106, 107n, 110, 110n, 111, 111n, 112, 112n, 113, 114, 115, 117, 118, 119, 121, 122, 124, 125, 127, 135, 136, 136n, 153

Hoehn, Edward—141n

Hudson, A. L.—32, 74n, 88, 88n, 103n

Jemison, J. H.—95, 95n, 96

Jones, Alonzo T.—30, 55, 58n, 63, 65, 66, 66n, 67, 68, 103, 154

Jorgensen, A. S.—144n

Karolyi, A. M.—107n

Kellogg, John Harvey—68

Kent, J. W.—128

Kluzit, Victor P.—134, 134n

LaRondelle, Hans K.—22, 22n, 23n, 102n, 104, 110, 112n, 117, 119, 135, 135n, 136, 136n, 140n

Lehman, J. W.—139, 139n, 140, 140n

Lowe, Harry W.—112n

MacGuire, Meade—71, 75n

Marter, E. W.—118n

Maxwell, C. Mervyn—125, 125n, 136n, 142

Maxwell, Lawrence—142n

McFarland, J. W.—138, 138n

Murdoch, W. G. C.—116, 116n

Naden, L. C.—103n, 106, 107n, 108, 108n, 112n, 113, 114n, 118n, 124

Neis, Richard—134, 134n

Neufeld, Don F.—125, 125n

Nichol, Francis D.—88n, 89n

Olson, A. V.—32, 58n, 59n, 64n, 70n,

73, 73n, 92, 92n

Olson, Robert W.—111n

Onjukka, Lauri—107n

Pease, Norval F.—32, 54, 54n, 55, 55n, 71, 71n, 72, 72n, 74, 74n, 75, 75n, 97, 97n, 112n, 144

Pierson, Robert H.—28n, 131, 132, 132n, 134, 137, 137n, 152n

Prescott, W. W.—19, 69, 75n

Price, George McCready—29n, 138, 138n

Read, W. E.—88

Reynolds, L. B.—118n

Ritchie, C. J.—118n

Ritz, Otto J.—89n

Rudy, H. L.—118, 118n

St. John, H. A.—70, 70n

Sargeant, E. N.—107n

Scherr, B. A—118n

Short, Donald K.—31, 32, 57n, 74, 87, 96n

Smith, Uriah—56, 56n, 57, 57n, 58n, 73, 73n, 154, 154n

Spalding, Arthur W.—31, 70, 70n, 76n, 96, 96n

Spangler, J. R.—138, 138n

Slade, Edwin Keck—71, 71n

Slade, John A.—107n

Standish, Russell R.—128n, 136n, 139, 139n, 144, 144n, 145

Starkey, Alan—109n, 118, 118n

Steinweg, Bruno William—31, 70, 70n, 71, 71n, 72, 72n

Thomson, G. B.—75n

Townend, M. G.—134, 134n

Tucker, J. L.—142, 142n

Vandeman, George—125n, 126n

Van Dolson, Leo—135n

Venden, Morris—143, 143n

Vick, E. W.—112n

Waggoner, E. J.—30, 55, 58n, 63, 64, 64n, 65, 65n, 66, 66n, 67, 67n, 68, 69, 69n, 70, 70n, 73, 91n, 103, 140, 154

Waggoner, J. H.—55, 56, 56n, 57, 70n, 92

Wallenkampf, Arnold V.—138, 138n

Watts, R. S.—112n, 113n, 115, 115n, 116, 116n, 118, 118n

Wheeler, E. E.—119, 119n

White, Ellen G.—12, 12n, 18, 19, 19n, 20, 23n, 24, 24n, 25, 25n, 26, 26n, 27, 30, 30n, 31, 31n, 33n, 54, 55, 59, 59n, 60, 60n, 61, 63, 64, 64n, 67, 67n, 73, 73n, 85, 86, 89n, 99, 99n, 152, 155, 155n, 156, 156n

White, James—55, 56, 56n, 59, 59n, 60, 60n

White, W. C.—70n

Wieland, Robert J.—31, 32, 33, 57n, 74, 86, 86n, 96n

Wilcox, M. C.—71, 71n, 72, 72n, 75n

Wilson, Neal C.—140, 140n

Wood, Kenneth H.—28n, 118, 118n, 124, 126n, 131, 131n, 132, 132n, 138, 138n

Yost, Frank H.—89n